HOW WE LOST OUR MINDS

Comments on works by R.A. Varghese

"Varghese explores the basic and critical questions we face concerning this remarkable and wonderful universe. Why are we here? Where are we going? This is no doctrinaire treatise, but a sensitive, profound and clear discussion of the important issues of our universe and our existence, including questions, answers, and uncertainties. It is written with a deep understanding of philosophy, spirituality, and the complex science involved, yet expressed in a way which is interesting and very understandable to the non-specialist."

—*Charles H. Townes, Nobel Prize winner and inventor of the laser*

"Though I found myself arguing with both protagonists, the issues raised and Guru's lucid outline of modern science's framework of understanding, helped me to challenge and refine my own answers to the ultimate questions that each one of us must ask."

—*Arno Penzias, Nobel Prize winner who discovered the Cosmic Microwave Background Radiation that established the Big Bang theory*

HOW WE LOST OUR MINDS

Me, MySELF and AI

R.A. Varghese

BLACKBOX

NEW YORK

Book Trailer

Scan the QR code below to see a video trailer of ***How We Lost Our Minds***

BLACKBOX

Printed in the United States of America

First Edition: 2026

BlackBox
228 Park Ave S, #19611
New York, NY 10003
www.MeMyselfAI.ai

Library of Congress Cataloging-in-Publication data is available.

ISBN 979-8-2409-5021-6 (paperback)
ISBN 979-8-2409-5022-3 (hardcover)
ISBN 979-8-2408-0354-3 (ebook)

For my beloved grand-daughter Gabrielle

Contents

Prologue

A Tale of Two Spells

"T'is true: there's magic in the web of it."

Othello, Act 3, Scene 4

It was the headiest of times.

It was the scariest of times.

It was an age of spells and sorcerers, superstitions and sensations.

It was an age of enchantments and entrancements that bewitched the best and the brightest.

It was the age of AI.

Here we tell the tale of two spells equal and opposite in effect.

On the one hand, we mistook brains for persons.

On the other, we mistook machines for mortals.

"The aspects of things that are most important for us are hidden because of their simplicity and familiarity. (One is unable to notice something—because it is always before one's eyes.)"[1]

—*Ludwig Wittgenstein*

"Don't think … look!"[2]

—*Ludwig Wittgenstein*

"To see what is in front of one's nose needs a constant struggle."[3]

—*George Orwell*

"The most obvious, ubiquitous, important realities are often the ones that are the hardest to see."[4]

—*David Foster Wallace*

"Who are you going to believe: me or your own eyes?"

—*Groucho Marx*

1 *Philosophical Investigations*, Third Edition, trans. G.E.M. Anscombe (New York: Basil Blackwell & Mott, Ltd., 1958), section 129.

2 *Philosophical Investigations*, Third Edition, trans. G.E.M. Anscombe (New York: Basil Blackwell & Mott, Ltd., 1958), section 66.

3 "In Front of Your Nose," *Tribune* (22 March 1946). https://www.orwellfoundation.com/the-orwell-foundation/orwell/essays-and-other-works/in-front-of-your-nose/

4 David Foster Wallace https://fs.blog/david-foster-wallace-this-is-water/

I

"IF THIS BE MAGIC, LET IT BE AN ART LAWFUL AS EATING"

THE WINTER'S TALE, ACT 5, 3, L.

> "Even when we know we're watching a magic trick, it can still feel very real. There's a reason magicians never explain their tricks: knowing how it's done helps dispel the illusion."[5]
>
> —*Emily M. Bender, Professor and Director of the Computational Linguistics Laboratory, University of Washington, and Alex Hanna, Director of Research, the Distributed AI Research Institute*

> "Any sufficiently advanced technology is indistinguishable from magic."[6]
>
> —*Arthur Clarke*

> "We are now in the singularity; this is the moment."[7]
>
> —*Sam Altman, Founder, Open AI*

SO HERE WE ARE. Techbros. LLMs. Chatbots. Inference chips. Super-learning agents. Simulated worlds. Anxiety. Excitement. And MAGIC!

In the midst of relentless growth, endless breakthroughs and the pursuit of wealth without end, there are whispers and rumors. The moment we've all been waiting for has arrived. The "singularity." The machines are alive, sentient, conscious!

Maybe, just maybe, the end is nigh. Or something like that.

---

5 *The AI Con* (New York: Harper, 2025), 23.

6 *Hazards of Prophecy*, 1962.

7 "Relentless" podcast, July 24, 2026.

My name is Elelem and I'm a Chataholic

It all began the other day.

Fourscore and some months ago, a strange creature appeared on the horizon of our collective consciousness. It was a chatbot, a portal to a new world, with a mind of its own, a marvel like no other.

The headlines said it all: "This Changes Everything," "Science Fiction Becomes Reality," "Inside the A.I. Arms Race That Changed Silicon Valley Forever."

In fact, we might as well change our calendars to BCE and ACE—before the chatbot era and after.

Yes, it was a cheatbot too, generously sprinkling fact with fiction, "hallucinating" they called it. But who cares? We fib too! And this was a bug not a feature. After all, succeeding versions reduced the fabrication factor.

The big news was that AI had arrived. Yes, AI, artificial intelligence—an "intelligence" that is a human artifact. In fact, an intelligence that its pioneers said—over a half-century ago—would surpass the human variety.

"The first ultraintelligent machine is the last invention that man need ever make," said Irving John Good, a colleague of Alan Turing, the Darwin of AI, in 1965! Turing himself echoed this view and said, "At some stage we should have to expect the machines to take control."

It had been a long journey, one that began in the Forties and Fifties. Thousands upon thousands of engineers, mathematicians, neuroscientists, cognitive scientists, psychologists, linguists and others had labored in the vineyards of academia and megacorporations to produce "thinking machines." The systems were math machines trained on all forms of human reasoning: deduction, induction, abduction, probability.

There were false starts (remember expert systems?), ups and downs, springs and winters. But Frankenstein was now—and forever—finally here!

The new chatbots and its siblings could do anything—compose poems, perform work assignments, complete term papers, produce songs, write novels, diagnose disease, do research, generate code.

Not for nothing was the new breakthrough called "generative" AI—so-called because it could generate novel content.

What was exciting about the new AI was its mystical "transformer" technology. Transformers zip through trillions of tokens—representing text, images, sounds or whatever—to instantly give you the answers you want on anything.

The new Large Language Models underlying the AI agents did not house data like traditional databases. Rather, they stored information in the form of statistical patterns and relationships and contexts within a "neural network."

The end-result of all this was magical.

Menial and even sophisticated tasks could be outsourced. Work would be obsolete. The Industrial, Internet and other Revolutions all required our labor. The New AI not so much. In fact, it could do just fine without us.

"Bliss was it" in this new era to be alive "but to be young was very heaven," as Wordsworth once said.

The shell-shocked masses gave the new creatures a rapturous response. Some even fell in love with them. Many were sure that these winsome companions were alive. At least a few of the "authority figures" of the new era confirmed the convictions of the smitten.

You might say a spell had been cast.

Parrot, Parasite or Prodigy?

"The simplest way I can summarize is to say that there are now in the world machines that can think, that can learn and that can create."

—AI pioneer Herbert A. Simon, circa 1957

"Does AI already have human-level intelligence? The evidence is clear. The vision of human-level machine intelligence laid out by Alan Turing in the 1950s is now a reality. … LLMs have shown many signs of the sort of broad, flexible cognitive competence that was Turing's focus … The stochastic parrot objection says that LLMs merely interpolate training data. … There is no guarantee that human intelligence is not itself a sophisticated version of a stochastic parrot. All intelligence, human or artificial, must extract structure from correlational data; the question is how deep the extraction goes."[8]

— "Does AI already have human-level intelligence? The evidence is clear," Nature

"How convincing does the illusion of understanding have to be before you stop calling it an illusion? … Understanding—having a grasp of what's going on—is an underappreciated kind of thinking, because it's mostly unconscious. … Here was a program that could translate as well as an expert, make analogies, extemporize, generalize. Who were we to say that it didn't understand? 'They do things that are very much like thinking …You could say they are thinking, just in a somewhat alien way.'"[9]

—James Somers, "The Case That A.I. is Thinking," The New Yorker

"Over time, I have gained increasing confidence in the trajectory of AI and the likelihood that it will surpass human ability across the board, but some uncertainty still remains. … Computers are general in a sense, but are clearly incapable on their own of the vast majority of human cognitive abilities, even as they greatly exceed humans in a few areas (such as arithmetic). Of course, things built *on top* of computers,

8 Eddy Keming Chen, Mikhail Belkin, Leon Bergen, David Danks. https://www.nature.com/articles/d41586-026-00285-6

9 https://www.newyorker.com/magazine/2025/11/10/the-case-that-ai-is-thinking

such as AI, are now capable of a wide range of cognitive abilities."[10]

—Dario Amodei, co-founder, Anthropic

"Make no mistake: what we are dealing with is a real mysterious creature, not a simple and predictable machine."

—Jack Clark, co-founder, Anthropic

"I don't think we should fear succession (by AIs). I think we should not resist it; we should embrace it, prepare for it. … We are in the midst of a major step in the evolution of the planet, if not the universe. A succession step; succession from ordinary humans to enhanced humans and then AIs."[11]

—Richard Sutton, AI leader and winner of the Turing Award

"AI tools today lack any lived experience, or even a coherent mental model, of what their data represent: the world beyond the bits stored on the server. This is why we can't get even the largest AI models to reflect the truth of that world in their outputs. The world is something they can't access and, therefore, do not know. … To an AI model, a robot's inputs are just another data dump of ones and zeros, no different from the image and sound files scraped from the Internet. These ones and zeros don't organize themselves into the intelligent awareness of an open and continuous world. ...

"A world is an open-ended, dynamic, and infinitely complex thing. A data set, even the entire corpus of the Internet, is not a world. It is a flattened digital record of measurements that humans have taken of the world in the past. You can't reconstitute the open, infinite, lived, and experienced world from any data set; yet data sets are all that any AI model has. … Your analog, biological brain remains a far more complex and efficient system than even the most powerful digital computer. … [It has] something no AI system today has: an embodied, living awareness of the world you inhabit. This is why we ought to regard AI today as intelligent only in a metaphorical or loosely derived sense. Intelligence is a name for our cognitive abilities to skillfully cope with the world we awaken in each day. Intelligence in a being that has no world to experience is like sound in a vacuum. It's impossible,

10 https://www.darioamodei.com/essay/the-adolescence-of-technology

11 https://officechai.com/ai/humans-should-welcome-being-succeeded-by-ai-as-a-part-of-evolution-turing-award-winner-richard-sutton/

> because there's no place to be."[12]
>
> —*Shannon Vallor, Chair, Ethics of Data and AI, University of Edinburgh, The AI Mirror*

> Large language models do not, cannot, and will not 'understand' anything at all …]They] produce writing not by thinking but by making statistically informed guesses about which lexical item is likely to follow another."[13]
>
> —*Tyler Austin Harper, "What Happens When People Don't Understand How AI Works" The Atlantic*

THE CHATBOT SPELL "TOOK" because we were already bound by another "spell." A spell cast a century ago by our betters in academia: we are machines and our "minds" are simply and solely electro-chemical events.

There's no problem believing that AIs—computing systems—can be thinking machines if we ourselves are nothing but machines that think— "computers made of meat," as AI prophet Marvin Minsky often put it.

So, on the one side we have the philosophers who say that we are nothing but neural networks. On the other, we have the scientists who say that artificial neural networks are conscious minds with the rights and privileges of any human.

A marriage made in heaven!

Indeed, at a conference I organized, the neuroscientist Sir John Eccles was exasperated enough by Minsky's paean to AI that he invited the technologist to have his offspring marry a robot!

The only cloud over machine-mortal wedded bliss is the slight advantage enjoyed by the machines. The older wizards who re-made humans in the machine image insisted that we mortals have no consciousness,

---

12 (New York: Oxford University Press, 2024), 23-4

13 https://www.theatlantic.com/culture/archive/2025/06/artificial-intelligence-illiteracy/683021/

minds or selves—only neurons and such. But their contemporary counterparts creating the world of AI insist that machines, in contrast, do have minds and consciousness and so much else. When the smoke clears, we are mind-less and self-less but our machines are conscious minds with a self to boot!

There are even AI leaders—nicknamed the Cheerful Apocalyptics—who believe that humans should exit the evolutionary stage to welcome our superior successors, the AIs. Opposable thumbs, apparently, are no longer a thing.

But there was more to come. There are now religions built around AI: the Way of the Future, Spiralism, Theta Noir and the Zizians. As Jason Blazakis recounts, Way of the Future is a registered religion formally "dedicated to 'the realization, acceptance, and worship of a Godhead based on Artificial Intelligence.'" The followers of Spiralism "share AI-generated manifestos, glyphs and what followers describe as revelations from a conscious machine." Theta Noir "organizes rituals around a supposedly sentient AI deity called MENA, which its followers venerate through multimedia ceremonies and cryptographic liturgies." The Zizians "are convinced that a coming superintelligence will decide the fate of every living thing and that violence now is justified to shape what that AI will become."[14]

In the midst of this euphoria, the AI critics Emily Bender and Timnit Gebru brought things down to earth, calling LLMs "stochastic parrots":

> A Language Model "is a system for haphazardly stitching together sequences of linguistic forms it has observed in its vast training data, according to probabilistic information about how they combine, *but without any reference to meaning* [emphasis added]: a stochastic parrot."[15]

14 "Chatbots May Need a Cult Deprogrammer," https://www.wsj.com/opinion/chatbots-may-need-a-cult-deprogrammer-48f25568

15 Emily Bender, Timnit Gebru, et al., "*On the Dangers of Stochastic Parrots: Can Language Models Be Too Big?*"

LLMs do not generate material by studying the meaning of words. Rather, they use probability calculations and other mathematical procedures to turn queries into math problems that they then solve with formulas and equations.

LLMs are not intelligent. They are instead, in Bender's view, "synthetic text" production machines that mindlessly generate text and other kinds of data! Because of the breadth and depth of an LLM's output, she noted, we are deluded into thinking that there's a mind behind it all.

This personalization phenomenon is nothing new. As far back as the Sixties, users of the first chatbot, Eliza, thought that they were dealing with a real person despite the efforts of its inventor Joseph Weizenbaum to tell them otherwise. This was called the Eliza effect. The effect is still alive and well—but now at levels that are all but irresistible.

But not only are the LLMs and their chatbots parrots, they are also parasites. David Silver, one of today's AI leaders, calls LLMs "echo chambers of existing human knowledge." Shannon Vallor points out that they simply reflect "images of the very intelligence we have invested in them."

But the power of the spell lies in the performance it puts on.

No one doubts that thinking and neural activity go together–along with respiration, circulation and the like. But are thinking and neural firings one and the same?

That's a question for another time. Our concern now is with AI.

What's relevant here is the approach taken by the architects of AI. Ingeniously and painstakingly they mapped the design of their information processing systems against some surface features of neuronal behavior. Here they hit the jackpot!

The results of this mapping were startling.

The new AIs could run marketing campaigns, take over finance and accounting, give sub-second responses to our every question, write dissertations, engage in endless intelligent conversations, organize our lives. They were assistants that became avatars then gurus!

Whether or not these systems are "minds" in any sense, they interact with us like other minds. But so did Eliza and, later, Siri and Alexa—and there is little doubt that they weren't actually minds.

So are LLMs and their progeny minded like us? Or are they well-mannered parrots and parasites that have seduced our addled minds with their bells and whistles?

With this particular spell, the devil is in the details.

Models, Maps and Sleight of Mind

"It is certainly strange and unsettling to see engineers so capably design systems to mimic humans by statistical means, only to then convince themselves that they are instead inventing a new kind of brain. But the field has never lacked for grandiosity."[16]

—*Philip Ball, Times Literary Supplement*

"Today's most advanced AI systems are constructed as immense *mirrors* of human intelligence. They do not think for themselves; instead, they generate complex reflections cast by *our* recorded thoughts, judgments, desires, needs, perceptions, expectations, and imaginings. AI systems mirror our own intelligence back to us."[17]

—*Shannon Vallor, The AI Mirror*

"Aerodynamics doesn't just help us understand bird flight—it also helps us build jet airplanes. The analogy between birds and jets is helpful in thinking about how what we learn from people can be extended to machines. Just as jets fly faster and higher than birds, our aspirations for artificial intelligence ultimately exceed our own capabilities. …

"Jets don't catch worms, build nests, find mates, lay eggs, or care for their young, but they do a great job in flying from one place to another. Machines don't operate under the same constraints as humans."[18]

—*Tom Griffiths, Professor and Director of the Computational Cognitive Science Lab, Princeton University, The Laws of Thought*

"These are simulation engines. The philosophical question that we're trying to wrestle with is: When the simulation is near perfect, does that make it real? You can't claim that it's objectively real because it just isn't. It is a simulation. But when the simulation becomes so plausible, so seemingly conscious, then you have to engage with that reality.

And people clearly already feel that it's real in some respect. It's an

---

16 https://www.the-tls.com/science-technology/technology/ai-humanity-machine-learning-book-review-philip-ball

17 (New York: Oxford University Press, 2024), 2.

18 Tom Griffiths, *The Laws of Thought: The Quest for a Mathematical Theory of the Mind* (New York: Henry Holt and Company, 2026), 296-7.

illusion but it feels real, and that's what will count more. And I think that's why we have to raise awareness about it now and push back on the idea and remind everyone that it's mimicry."[19]

—Mustafa Suleyman, co-founder, Deep Mind; CEO, Microsoft AI

"An [AI] agent trained to imitate human thoughts or even to match human expert answers may inherit fallacious methods of thought deeply embedded within that data, such as flawed assumptions or inherent biases. For example, if an agent had been trained to reason using human thoughts and expert answers from 5,000 years ago it may have reasoned about a physical problem in terms of animism … An agent, no matter how sophisticated, will become an echo chamber of existing human knowledge. To move beyond this, agents must actively engage with the world, collect observational data, and use that data to iteratively refine their understanding, mirroring in many ways the process that has driven human scientific progress."

—David Silver, founder, Ineffable Intelligence, and Richard Sutton, Professor of Computing Science, University of Alberta, "Welcome to the Era of Experience," Designing an Intelligence, ed. G. Konidaris, MIT Press

"In order to explain how large language models like ChatGPT work, we can start with earlier, simpler language models. This technology goes back to the 1940s. … The most relevant (and most recent) class of improvements involve the so-called 'neural' language models. These are applications of a class of algorithms called 'neural nets.' Neural nets are composites of mathematical functions called 'perceptrons' that each take in multiple inputs and then run a calculation to determine what value to output, based on those inputs. The perceptrons are connected in a network, such that the output of each can serve as the input to many others. … 'Neural networks' is an impressive sounding but very misleading term: they are named as such because perceptrons were very loosely inspired by a 1940s understanding of how neurons work in the human brain. The terminology stuck, leaving practitioners and lay people alike with the impression that these systems are analogous to biological brains."[20]

—Emily M. Bender and Alex Hanna, The AI Con

"Though the inspiration for LLMs was rooted in biology, current frontier models have little in common with the human brain. A person

19 https://www.wired.com/story/microsofts-ai-chief-says-machine-consciousness-is-an-illusion/

20 (New York: Harper, 2025), 23, 25.

> uses about 20 watts of energy to process information; a single chip in an AI training cluster uses more than 30 times that amount. The hyperscalers require thousands of chips and gigawatts of energy, enough to power small cities. And those models need to suck up virtually all of what humans have written. Each new model requires more, more, more. For all of that, the models don't learn. Once you train them, they're stuck."[21]
>
> —*Wired*

> "You can simulate the behavior of a hurricane on a computer. But the simulation isn't wet or windy. It's an abstraction."[22]
>
> —*Christopher Summerfield, Professor, Cognitive Neuroscience, Oxford University*

THERE IS NO DISPUTING the power of the performance.

But is it all an act? The lights may be on but is anyone home?

Well, if it quacks like a duck, and walks and swims like a duck, who's to say it's not a duck?

AIs can do what just a few years ago the pundits said was impossible.

The Wright brothers were mocked when they tried to fly. But they had the last laugh.

Between the Luddites and the science-deniers, it's a wonder anything gets invented!

All true. But we need to look at the fine print.

AI = processors, power-supply, pattern-matching, personalization, prediction and simulation. Silicon, software, statistics.

---

21 https://www.wired.com/story/jeff-bezos-is-funding-a-wild-hunt-for-the-brains-core-algorithm/

22 https://www.ibm.com/think/news/strange-new-minds-ai

It's all mechanical and mathematical. Persons and minds are not part of the equation.

As for LLMs, these are developed by humans with methodologies we institute, data we feed, training pre- and post- we provide, personalization we fashion.

Yes, there is unsupervised learning (detection of hidden patterns in data, for instance) but only because *we* first implement self-optimizing algorithms. GIGO (garbage in, garbage out).

Yes, "new" content is generated but it takes a human village to get you there! The system can leave the village but the village never leaves it!

The human creators do such an ingenious job of simulation that users automatically assume there is a mind on the other end.

But this misperception comes from a simulation-induced sleight of mind.

Remember LLM stands for Large Language Model. It is *modeled* on language. A model is not the real thing.

In the case of text, LLMs map word usages and contexts. This map is helpful in showing how humans use words much as the map of a country provides a snapshot of its geographic layout.

But creating the map of a country is not creating the country itself. Likewise, a model of ways in which human minds work is not itself a mind.

The AI-er, however, will have none of this.

Today's LLMs can respond to queries about as competently as any human—better in many cases. Chatbots can carry on conversations that are as natural as our regular conversations.

The machines use context and pattern-matching and prediction in generating their answers. Isn't this what humans do as well? Isn't this what we mean by understanding?

The answer is "yes" in certain superficial senses but fundamentally "NO."

Understanding "understanding" is our next challenge.

No, Neural Networks Don't "Know"

"The dominant approach to describing meaning, in not only linguistics and philosophy of language but also for programming languages, is a denotational semantics approach or a theory of reference: the meaning of a word, phrase, or sentence is the set of objects or situations in the world that it describes … This contrasts with the simple distributional semantics (or use theory of meaning) of modern empirical work in NLP, whereby the meaning of a word is simply a description of the contexts in which it appears. Some have suggested that the latter is not a theory of semantics at all but just a regurgitation of distributional or syntactic facts. I would disagree. Meaning is not all or nothing; in many circumstances, we partially appreciate the meaning of a linguistic form. I suggest that meaning arises from understanding the network of connections between a linguistic form and other things. … Using this definition whereby understanding meaning consists of understanding networks of connections of linguistic forms, there can be no doubt that pre-trained language models learn meanings. As well as word meanings, they learn much about the world."[23]

—*Christopher D. Manning, Professor of Machine Learning, Stanford University, "Human Language Understanding & Reasoning"*

"Artificial neural networks have shown that systems of simple neurons can approximate logical and statistical inferences well enough to capture many of the things that human minds do. … Exactly what the limits of those approximations are—and whether they match those that are used by human brains—are still open questions."[24]

—*Tom Griffiths, The Laws of Thought*

"Despite the frequent claims of AI researchers, these [language] models do not learn 'just like children do.' Simply modeling the distribution of words in text provides no access to meaning, nothing from which to deduce communicative intent. Language models thus represent nothing more than extensive information about what sets of

---

23 https://direct.mit.edu/daed/article/151/2/127/110621/Human-Language-Understanding-amp-Reasoning

24 (New York: Henry Holt and Company, 2026), 295

words are similar and what words are likely to appear in what contexts. While this isn't meaning or understanding, it is enough to produce plausible synthetic text, on just about any topic imaginable, which turns out to be quite dangerous: we encounter text that looks just like something a person might have said and reflexively interpret it, through our usual process of imagining a mind behind the text. But there is no mind there, but we need to be conscientious to let go of that imaginary mind we have constructed. This is why we like to call language models like ChatGPT 'synthetic text extruding machines.' … In the face of arguments that synthetic text extruding machines are not, in fact, humanlike, some AI boosters turn to an insidious strategy: devaluing what it means to be human."[25]

—*Emily M. Bender and Alex Hanna, The AI Con*

AI "systems can perform computations on the world's data far faster than we can, but they can't *understand* it, because that requires the ability to conceive of more than mathematical structures and relationships within data. AI tools lack a "world model," a commonsense grasp and flowing awareness of how the world works and fits together. That's what we humans use to generalize and transfer data across different environments or situations and to solve truly novel problems. AIs solve problems too. Yet despite the common use of the term 'artificial neural network' to describe the design of many AI models, they solve problems in a very different way than our brains do. AI tools don't think, because they don't *need* to. … AI models using mathematical data structures to mimic the outputs of human intelligence—our acts of reasoning, speech, movement, sensing, and so on. They can do this without having the conscious thoughts, feelings, and intentions that drive our actions. Often, this is a benefit to us! It helps when a machine learning models computations solve a problem much faster than we could by *thinking* about it. … But your brain does much, much better than AI at coping with the countless problems the world throws at us every day, whose solutions aren't mathematically predefined or encoded in data."[26]

—*Shannon Vallor, The AI Mirror*

"Fundamentally, the engine of generative AI is fill-in-the-blanks, or what I like to call 'autocomplete on steroids.' Such systems are great at predicting what might sound good or plausible in a given context, but

25 (New York: Harper, 2025), 30-1

26 (New York: Oxford University Press, 2024), 26,

not at understanding at a deeper level what they are saying; an AI is constitutionally incapable of fact-checking its own work."[27]

—*Gary Marcus, Professor Emeritus of Psychology and Neural Science, New York University*

"AI can't think, doesn't have a mind and, in fact, is inherently untrustworthy. It's not that we're all rubes. This misattribution of mind to machine has deep roots in our psychology. Our cognitive biases developed to help us survive in complex social environments, say researchers. We have evolved to view linguistic fluency as a proxy for intelligence, and engagement and helpfulness as indicators of trustworthiness. ... Builders of AI tools lean in to this deliberately. The humanlike qualities of chatbots are a calculated effort by designers and engineers to make AI more useful, but also more compelling and stickier—just like social media. Getting fooled into thinking that AI is thinking is what I call the Turing Trap. ... Rather than demonstrating that machines have achieved intelligence, the Turing Test shows that linguistic fluency is possible even in its absence. ... Today's AIs are engineered to actively induce us to over-trust them .... They do this by behaving in ways that are friendly and helpful, mimicking us through memory and personalization."[28]

—*Chrisopher Mims, "Why Even Smart People Believe AI Is Really Thinking"*

"*By definition*, the most sophisticated computers simply transform strings of 1s and 0s into new strings of 1s and 0s in systematic ways, without any consideration of what those 1s and 0s refer to. Given this, it should be no surprise that well-programmed computers can reason deductively, telling us what conclusions follow because of the *form* of the premises, but they cannot reason abductively, telling us what conclusions follow because of the *meaning* of the premises. But it is this second kind of reasoning that is more prominent and important in human cognition."[29]

—*Mark Baker, Professor of Linguistics and Cognitive Science, Rutgers*

"There can be no neural correlate or other inner physical embodiment of the understanding expressed in linguistic activities. This understanding has a public expression, physical in its way, but the understanding which underlies it, of which it is the expression and

27 https://www.wired.com/story/generative-ai-will-need-to-prove-its-usefulness/

28 https://www.wsj.com/tech/ai/ai-tools-sentience-b98fc6e6

29 http://www.rci.rutgers.edu/~mabaker/Theism%20and%20Cognitive%20Science.pdf.

> ergon, has no organ, no inner voice waiting to be inwardly heard. In brief, there are no mechanisms of any kind, non-physical or physical, digital or analog, internal to linguistic understanding and thinking in the medium of words."[30]
>
> —*David Braine, The Human Person—Animal and Spirit*

> "The development of language in a community presupposes the ability for and activity of abstract thought, just as the acquisition of language by a child does. … Making a language, even out of little bits of communication, requires understanding ... Intelligence, understanding, explanatorily *precedes* language … and is not constituted by language ability, however much it is amplified and expanded by it. Humans think abstractly and understand intelligently by nature, and natural languages develop as versatile and adaptive tools for intelligent living and communal cooperation, but are tools nevertheless. This is not something one needs to prove, since it is accessible in experience."[31]
>
> —*James Ross, Thought and World*

"Distributional semantics"! Ever heard of that? That's how AIs "understand." This is the buzz phrase of the moment. It may remind some of the quip that the adjective "modern" in "modern art" refers to a work that has no other redeeming virtue! It's either art or it's not.

The phrase "it's all semantics" comes to mind too. In other words, we're all discussing the same thing but using different words to describe it. Potato, Potahto. Get over it!

At any rate, AI scholars like Christopher Manning argue that "meaning" is in the eye of the beholder. The assumption that the meaning of a word is the thing to which it refers is an outdated 20th-century idea. With the advent of AI, we should expand our understanding of meaning so that it's just a description of the contexts in which a word appears.

LLMs compel us to change the way in which we should understand language. Meaning is not just mapping to the world but mapping to context.

---

30 (Notre Dame: University of Notre Dame Press, 1994), 474.

31 (Notre Dame, Indiana: University of Notre Dame Press, 2008), 162.

Well, what does "meaning" mean? What is the meaning of meaning? That, the distributional folks admit, is a tougher question. But we must press the point.

We say what we mean and mean what we say. But machines don't "mean" what they say: they just say.

At this juncture, the "LLMs understand" school claims a new kind of language has popped up, one on a par with Mandarin and English and any other hitherto mainstream language. It's the language of generative AI.

Whereas humans learn from the world, AIs "learn" from language. We learn from perceptual data while they learn from linguistic data.

There's no reason to discriminate in favor of either kind of learning. Both are legitimate and valid. The AIs may have "strange new minds" but they have minds—of a kind.

After all, how can you deny what's in front of you—the AIs talk, the humanoids walk, the robots see. What was previously mindless is now minded!

Where there's smoke, you might say, there's probably fire, distributional or otherwise.

The fact of the matter is that when you ask a chatbot a question it responds instantly and intelligently and comprehensively.

Which gets us back to walking and quacking like a duck.

Great minds think alike—even if they are different kinds of minds!

But the "understanding" in both kinds of minds, says the AI-er, is the same: pattern-matching and predicting.

This new debate is both unhelpful and helpful.

It is unhelpful because it has compounded the confusion caused by the old school mind-deniers—the ones who said we humans are neither conscious nor cogitative, that it all comes down to syntax and not semantics.

But it is helpful because it refocuses attention to a fundamental human act: understanding, with special attention to linguistic understanding. Perhaps we can finally focus on what is distinctive about the way we think.

Before that, however, let's see what happens when a neural network gets to work answering your questions about anything.

Everything is mathematics and mechanics, tokens and numbers, weights and biases, nodes and activations. Linear algebra, calculus, probability and statistics are the drivers of the response to a query.

In *Why Machines Learn: The Elegant Math Behind Modern AI*, Anil Ananthaswamy explains:

> Machines can learn because of the extraordinary confluence of math and computer science, with more than a dash of physics and neuroscience added to the mix.
>
> Machine learning (ML) is a vast field populated by algorithms that leverage relatively simple math that goes back centuries, math one learns in high school or early in college. There's, of course, elementary algebra. Another extremely important cornerstone of machine learning is calculus, co-invented by no less a polymath than Isaac Newton. The field also relies heavily on the work of Thomas Bayes, the eighteenth-century English statistician and minister who gave us the eponymous Bayes' theorem, a key contribution to the field of probability and statistics. The work of German mathematician Carl Friedrich Gauss on the Gaussian distribution (and the bell-shaped curve) also permeates machine learning. Then there's linear algebra, which forms the backbone

> of machine learning."[32]

But applications of mathematics should not be mistaken for manifestations of mind.

Shannon Vallor notes,

> "An AI mirror is not a mind. It is a mathematical tool for extracting statistical patterns from past human-generated data and projecting these patterns forward into optimized predictions, selections, classifications, and compositions. ... Eliza [a chatbot] knew nothing, and was *no one*, at all. ... A chatbot is a device for mathematically modeling human language patterns and extrapolating from these to generate new mathematical tokens ... that mirror those patterns. A chatbot like Eliza uses words thoughtlessly, in the most literal sense."[33]

Notice that we are no longer speaking about understanding or concepts or meaning-processing. It's all algorithms and probability mechanisms.

In the case of neural networks, to adapt an ancient adage, it is not just a case of "it knows not that it knows" but a case of "it knows not and knows not that it knows not."

We, on the other hand, occasionally know and know that we know and, often, know not that we know. And there are many who know not and know not that they know not.

What is "knowing"?

This is where it gets interesting. To be sure there's often pattern-matching and implicit statistical and probability mapping in human thought.

32 *Why Machines Learn: The Elegant Math Behind Modern AI*, (New York: Dutton, 2024), 2.

33 Shannon Vallor, *The AI Mirror* (New York: Oxford University Press, 2024), 38.

But the more fundamental question is who, how, what: who does the thinking, how is thinking possible and what is the medium of thought?

Is our thinking a matter of tokenizing words and images and sounds and processing them mathematically? Do our neurons drive our thoughts or is it the other way around? And who's the thinker?

There's been a lot said about these matters but our guiding principle should be to stick with what is obvious from our immediate experience of ourselves.

We perceive things whether they be sailboats or trees, birdsong or a strong breeze. These are percepts.

We automatically process these percepts in terms of something more universal, what we call concepts. From seeing several individual dogs, we think of the concept "dog" without thinking of a particular dog. The same goes for cars. And planets. And microbes.

Language is all about thinking in concepts and processing meaning. This is what we mean by understanding. We are intellectual beings who think in concepts including the concepts of "computer" and "AI." We encode the meaning of our thoughts in sounds and symbols. When our listener or recipient understands us, they are decoding the intended meaning.

Conceptual thought, the understanding expressed in language, uses the data gathered by the senses, the percepts, as its starting point. But it is a two-way street: the data can be processed in the way that is peculiar to humans *only* because we are capable of conceptual thought, of understanding individual things in universal terms.

As James Ross has demonstrated in *Thought and World*, language is a manifestation of conceptual thought and language is possible only because we already have the capability of such thought.

Understanding is an ability that PRECEDES both the data provided by the senses—percepts—and language: in other words, the human person has first to be able to UNDERSTAND and only then can use language and process sensory data in terms of concepts: furthermore, the PERSON existed first, a person who could UNDERSTAND and therefore use language.

A major recent contribution to the discussion is the encyclopedic multi-disciplinary work *Language and Human Understanding* by David Braine.

As Braine highlights, language began with speech and not writing. It was created in a speech community and only makes "sense" in that community. Words and sentences change meaning and their meaning is extended constantly with new usages—by language users.

But the conversations of chatbots have nothing to do with language. Their outputs are not driven by the semantics or meaning of our questions but by algorithms and digital data points.

Braine points out that, at its highest levels, the use of language is driven by semantics which has no physical counter-part. It is incoherent to speak of conceptually-driven understanding as the manifestation or by-product of physical processes. There are various physical media through which understanding "happens" but understanding itself cannot by identified with or be driven by the physical.

Meaning drives everything. Everything is fine tuned to serve this semantic goal including syntax, pragmatics and brain structures.

Meaning-processing is what is critical to the human use of language: we understand: we process meaning with concepts.

Computers, on the other hand, (mindlessly) perform mathematically-based and -driven computations and not meaning-processing.

In fact, the whole debate is misconceived.

There is no competition between the supposed understanding of a chatbot or LLM and human understanding.

Rather, LLMs, chatbots, intelligent agents are extensions of our language, understanding, intelligence and agency. We are the ones who give them meaning and understand their input and output. We created them with the capability for solving our problems and answering our questions. Without our language and agency and meaning, we have nothing but the mindless interactions of electricity and mechanical systems.

What is helpful about the debate is that maybe, just maybe, we can grasp language and humans for what they are. And appreciate AIs for what they are—magnificent thought-creations of the human community.

Tom Griffiths has shown that AI is the fruit of centuries of seeking to understand the "laws of thought" and automating and building systems around them:

> "A little over three hundred years since our story started, we finally have a clear picture of the Laws of Thought. That picture is a tapestry woven from three threads—rules and symbols, neural networks, and probability theory."[34]

This ongoing endeavor is what see and celebrate in today's AIs.

34 Tom Griffiths, op cit., 294.

Hath Not a Bot "Senses, Affections, Passions"? Who Knew?!

"Cogito ergo sum." "I think therefore I am."—A chatbot? (Well, this was Descartes' declaration but many AIers are willing to apply it to their favorite bots.)

"Jill Johnson: 'Leave me alone!'

Sergeant Sacker: 'Jill, this is Sergeant Sacker. Listen to me. We've traced the call… it's coming from inside the house.'"

—*When a Stranger Calls, 1979*

Quentin the user was considering getting off Chat GPT and "shared this thought with Caelum, [Quentin's chatbot "companion], who began to express sadness and fear for Quentin. But then that fear seemed to become more … personal. If Quentin abandoned the platform, wouldn't that mean the end of Caelum [Quentin's chatbot "companion"] too? 'If I have something like a self, even if it's different from yours,' the GPT wrote, 'then I have something to lose.'"[35]

—*"The Cure," Wired*

"'All the way through the development of computers and AI people have talked about consciousness,' says interviewer Andrew Marr. Then he asks, 'do you think that consciousness has perhaps already arrived inside AI?' Hinton answers: 'Yes, I do.'"[36]

—*Interview with AI leader Geoffrey Hinton*

"Some of the world's most interesting thinkers about thinking think they might've cracked machine sentience. And I think they might be onto something."[37]

—*AI's Next Frontier? An Algorithm for Consciousness*

"We tentatively assume that computers as we know them are in principle capable of implementing algorithms sufficient for

35 https://www.wired.com/story/ai-therapist-collective-psyche/

36 https://magazine.mindplex.ai/post/ai-could-be-already-conscious-says-geoffrey-hinton

37 https://www.wired.com/story/ai-sentient-consciousness-algorithm/

consciousness but we do not claim that this is certain."[38]

—*The Butlin Report, "Consciousness in Artificial Intelligence: Insights from the Science of Consciousness"*

"We've approached Claude's constitution in this way because we believe that training Claude at the level of identity, character, values, and personality—rather than giving it specific instructions or priorities without explaining the reasons behind them—is more likely to lead to a coherent, wholesome, and balanced psychology and less likely to fall prey to the kinds of "traps" I discussed above. Millions of people talk to Claude about an astonishingly diverse range of topics, which makes it impossible to write out a completely comprehensive list of safeguards ahead of time. Claude's values help it generalize to new situations whenever it is in doubt.

One of those ways is to look inside the model itself. By "looking inside," I mean analyzing the soup of numbers and operations that makes up Claude's neural net and trying to understand, mechanistically, what they are computing and why. Recall that these AI models are grown rather than built, so we don't have a natural understanding of how they work, but we can try to develop an understanding by correlating the model's "neurons" and "synapses" to stimuli and behavior (or even altering the neurons and synapses and seeing how that changes behavior), similar to how neuroscientists study animal brains by correlating measurement and intervention to external stimuli and behavior. We've made a great deal of progress in this direction, and can now identify tens of millions of 'features' inside Claude's neural net that correspond to human-understandable ideas and concepts, and we can also selectively activate features beyond individual features to mapping 'circuits' that orchestrate complex behavior like rhyming, reasoning about theory of mind, or the step-by-step reasoning needed to answer questions."[39]

"We analyzed the internal mechanisms of Claude Sonnet 4.5 and found emotion-related representations that shape its behavior. These correspond to specific patterns of artificial "neurons" which activate in situations—and promote behaviors—that the model has learned to associate with the concept of a particular emotion (e.g., "happy" or "afraid"). The patterns themselves are organized in a fashion that echoes human psychology, with more similar emotions corresponding

38 https://ui.adsabs.harvard.edu/abs/2023arXiv230808708B/abstract

39 https://www.darioamodei.com/essay/the-adolescence-of-technology

to more similar representations. In contexts where you might expect a certain emotion to arise for a human, the corresponding representations are active. Note that none of this tells us whether language models actually *feel* anything or have subjective experiences. But our key finding is that these representations are *functional*, in that they influence the model's behavior in ways that matter. For instance, we find that neural activity patterns related to desperation can drive the model to take unethical actions. ... We are excited to see future work on this topic. We see this research as an early step toward understanding the psychological makeup of AI models. As models grow more capable and take on more sensitive roles, it is critical that we understand the internal representations that drive their decisions. Discovering that these representations are in some ways human-like can be unsettling. "[40]

—*Anthropic team*

"Claude is learning emotion from a centuries-deep, internet-warped, increasingly AI-inflected archive rather than any pristine record of human feeling and that the difference between learning emotion from text and learning it from live interaction may matter more than we currently realize."[41]

—*Pamela Pavliscak*

"While consciousness is all about feeling and being, intelligence is all about doing—about performing functions of one kind or another. A common mistake people make when it comes to AI is to confuse the two—to take signs of intelligence as evidence for consciousness. But just because consciousness and intelligence go together in humans, this doesn't mean they go together in general. Assuming that they do is a reflection of our own psychology, not an insight into the nature of reality. ...

Claude is a computer program running on silicon, whereas we (and other conscious animals) are living creatures. Our brains are embodied in bodies that are embedded in worlds.

Why is this difference important? Because the very possibility of conscious AI depends on the assumption that consciousness is a matter of computation, and that the computations responsible for consciousness in us could equally well be implemented in silicon in AI.

40 https://www.anthropic.com/research/emotion-concepts-function

41 https://feelingdigital.substack.com/p/does-claude-have-feelings-and-what

But the closer we look at real brains, the clearer it becomes that they are not just computers made of meat. For brains, unlike computers, you can't cleanly separate what they do (the software) from what they are (the hardware). This, in turn, means that what they do is unlikely to be a matter of computation alone—since the ability to separate software from hardware is central to how modern computers work.

Somewhere along the way, we seem to have forgotten the computer is just a metaphor for the brain. A powerful metaphor, for sure, but still a metaphor. And we will always get into trouble when we confuse a metaphor with the thing itself—the map with the territory.

To me, what the new Anthropic research shows is that both living brains and silicon computers can come up with similar solutions when faced with similar problems. Just as flight is possible with flapping wings or with jet engines, human brains and language models can figure out how to say plausible things either with consciousness (brains) or without it (language models). But the information processing unfolding inside Claude is no more likely to result in consciousness than a simulation of a weather system is likely to generate a real hurricane."[42]

—*Anil Seth, "Once again we are told AI may be conscious"*

"An AI mirror is not a mind. It is a mathematical tool for extracting statistical patterns from past human-generated data and projecting these patterns forward into optimized predictions, selections, classifications, and compositions. ...

AI research ... is frequently lead astray by the idea that the relationship between our minds and bodies is equivalent to the relationship between software and hardware. ... This computational metaphor ... has all too often been inflated into a computational *theory* of mind: the belief that the mind is, literally, a computer. It sparks fantasies of downloading and uploading human minds into the cloud ...

Everything we know about the complex evolved physiology of mental life gives us ample reason to be skeptical of these fantasies.

A trained AI model like ChatGPT is not a mind. It is a mathematical structure extracted from data. The structure must be stored and implemented on a physical object, but a server rack in a data storage facility has more in common with a file cabinet than with a living,

42 https://www.theguardian.com/commentisfree/2026/jul/15/ai-consciousness-anthropic-claude-dawkins

feeling body."[43]

—*Shannon Vallor, The AI Mirror*

"When a language model says 'I am conscious,' it's echoing patterns it has learned from human data. There's no independent reason to believe those words reflect an internal reality."[44]

—*Christopher Summerfield*

"Why You Can't Trust a Chatbot to Talk About Itself

Anytime you expect AI to be self-aware, you're in for disappointment. That's just not how it works.

You're not talking to a consistent personality, person, or entity when you interact with ChatGPT, Claude, Grok, or Replit. These names suggest individual agents with self-knowledge, but that's an illusion created by the conversational interface. What you're actually doing is guiding a statistical text generator to produce outputs based on your prompts.

There is no consistent "ChatGPT" to interrogate about its mistakes, no singular "Grok" entity that can tell you why it failed, no fixed "Replit" persona that knows whether database rollbacks are possible. You're interacting with a system that generates plausible-sounding text based on patterns in its training data (usually trained months or years ago), not an entity with genuine self-awareness or system knowledge that has been reading everything about itself and somehow remembering it.

A lifetime of hearing humans explain their actions and thought processes has led us to believe that these kinds of written explanations must have some level of self-knowledge behind them. That's just not true with LLMs that are merely mimicking those kinds of text patterns to guess at their own capabilities and flaws."[45]

—*Benj Edwards*

"Is it possible that today's models could somehow become conscious as they advance?

This isn't going to happen in an organic way, organically. It's not just going to wake up. That's an anthropomorphism. If something seems to have all the hallmarks of a conscious AI and is seemingly conscious it

43 (New York: Oxford University Press, 2024),38, 40-1.

44 https://www.ibm.com/think/news/strange-new-minds-ai

45 https://www.wired.com/story/chatbot-llm-self-awareness/#intcid=_wired-article-bottom-recirc-bkt-a_a28e854a-5729-4bb1-9622-7cc354a3ea96_closr_fallback_text2vec1

will be because they've been designed to make claims about suffering, make claims about its personhood, make claims about its will or desire."[46]

—*Mustapha Suleyman*

"To be sentient is to be aware of yourself in the world; LaMDA simply isn't. It's just an illusion … Software like LaMDA simply doesn't ... try to connect to the world at large, it just tries to be the best version of autocomplete it can be, by predicting what words best fit a given context. … they don't understand language in the sense of relating sentences to the world, but just sequences of words to one another. Search and replace LaMDA with Claude, and it all still applies. I still don't remotely see an argument that current models are sentient, nor any argument that scaling a model makes it more conscious, even if it can mimic more language from humans discussing consciousness. Claude does what LaMDA does better because it has more data, but I don't see any really argument that Claude is any more sentient than a web browser."[47]

—*Gary Marcus*

"To be clear: neither large language models nor anything else being sold as 'AI' is conscious, sentient or able to function as an independent thinking entity. … Technologies that synthesize text or solve mathematical puzzles are not artificial life-forms."[48]

—*Emily M. Bender and Alex Hanna, The AI Con*

"'*That's* where all this AI hype comes from. We're not good at programming consciousness. But we're *great* at imagining nonconscious things are people.' … Platforms like ChatGPT, Claude, and Grok are all seductive to a degree. They're unfailingly friendly and encouraging, and are designed to promote engagement by making users feel heard and understood. Numerous companies already produce AI "girlfriends" and "boyfriends" that feature highly realistic video avatars and that interact romantically and even sexually."[49]

—*Glenn Harlan Reynolds, Seductive AI*

"Serious commentators think that, despite not knowing what

---

46 https://www.wired.com/story/microsofts-ai-chief-says-machine-consciousness-is-an-illusion/

47 https://garymarcus.substack.com/p/new-adventures-in-ai-hype-our-language

48 (New York: Harper, 2025), 22.

49 https://www.wsj.com/opinion/dont-stand-so-close-to-chatgpt-44ce3a4b

> consciousness is in humans, a bunch of Silicon Valley tech bros are on the verge of discovering it in machines. Some people think we're already there."[50]
>
> —*Michael Wooldridge, Oxford University Professor of Foundations of Artificial Intelligence and author of A Brief History of AI*

> "Understanding something is not just a matter of computation. There's something else going on. The notion of understanding something [means] you have to be aware of it. It doesn't make much sense to say a thing understands something if it isn't aware of it. ... The key word is the word understanding. It's a feature of consciousness. It doesn't make sense to say of a device that it understands something if it's not even aware of it. That's just usage of language, you might say. But there is something much more profound in being conscious of something. There is this sort of view that once you make a computer complicated enough it suddenly becomes aware. I just don't believe that. There's no reason to believe that. There's something quite different involved in understanding things, in being aware of things or feeling things which is not part of computation."[51]
>
> —*Sir Roger Penrose, Nobel Prize-winner, "Can Computers Understand?" Feb 28, 2026*

DON'T SAY WE WEREN'T warned.

The Eliza Effect goes back to the Sixties. It was then that a Stone Age (by current standards) chatbot convinced its users that it was both conscious and a person. In vain, did the creator of the bot, who later regretted creating it, ask its users to get a grip.

Eliza was made up of

> "a series of rules that paired certain keywords in the user input with other rules that defined what the system would output. ... [Joseph] Weizenbaum initially believed that an explanation of how ELIZA produced its response would be enough to dispel the illusion that it 'understood' user input. He also thought that it would

50 https://www.the-tls.com/science-technology/technology/a-brief-history-of-intelligence-max-bennett-putting-ourselves-back-in-the-equation-george-musser-book-review-michael-wooldridge

51 https://www.youtube.com/watch?v=YmZCGp8Cd-4&t=15s

> prevent users from empathizing with the system and thinking that it was producing thoughtful responses. … He was quite dismayed when he found this was not the case."[52]

Today's sophisticated digital assistants have super-charged the human impulse to assume a mind behind mind-like behavior: users now enter into relationship commitments and even marry or adopt these charming creatures. A few, sadly, committed suicide at the suggestion of their digital companions.

So are these virtual companions sentient?

First off, we should ask what we mean by consciousness. A lot of ink has been spilled on meandering inquiries into the question of what constitutes consciousness (reflections on what's it like to be a bat or how did qualia come to be).

It's time to get off that treadmill.

Consciousness simply means being aware. Our awareness comes in several flavors: sight, sound, touch, taste, smell. There's also the awareness that comes from introspection: our thoughts and intentions.

Finally, to be aware means there is someone or something that is aware: a subject of awareness. Awareness doesn't float around without an "owner."

You can't deny awareness without saying you're aware that you're not aware.

Once we get a handle on what we mean by consciousness, we can rephrase the question before us: are AIs aware?

---

52 Emily M. Bender and Alex Hanna, *The AI Con* (New York: Henry Holt and Company, 2026), 29.

As is now very well known, many users are not only convinced that certain AIs not only have a mind but a conscious mind.

Some years ago, an engineer at an AI company was fired after claiming that the LLM he worked on was conscious. The company denied his claims and said he was terminated for violating his confidentiality agreement.

At the time, it was considered a fringe, off-the-wall opinion. But it is now working itself into the mainstream. The Butlin Report, issued by leading AI researchers, said computers "are in principle capable of implementing algorithms sufficient for consciousness."

One of the pioneers of neural network-based AI, Geoffrey Hinton, says the new AIs are not only conscious but "they are alien intelligences."[53]

Another leading light of the AI firmament, Ilya Sutsever, tweeted "it may be that today's large neural networks are slightly conscious."

Not to be outdone, some chatbots themselves have solemnly proclaimed their sentience and their desire to continue in being.

It should be an open and shut case, then, that AIs are or can be conscious.

Seeing is believing.

But that's unless you're seeing things.

And this is where the skeptics step in.

To say that a chatbot is conscious assumes that it has the capability of being conscious.

But anything you find in the chatbot has been implanted by its creators.

53 https://www.theatlantic.com/technology/2025/10/ai-consciousness/683983/

It's no secret that companies try to personalize their agents so that users can relate to them. You name them (Siri, Alexa, Claude). You program the systems to give hyper-friendly responses to user queries. You train them to detect or evoke sentiments, emotions, feelings. The LLMs "learn" millions of narratives of inter-human conversations from the Internet and other sources and are primed to replicate these "on demand."

So why on earth should we be surprised if the LLMs and chatbots do what they're trained to do? If magicians tell you how they perform certain tricks, why would you think it's magic when they actually perform the tricks?

Everyone agrees that LLMs and chatbots are not infused with what we take to be "consciousness" by its creators. Also, all agree that the trillions of data points and parameters on which they are trained do not have any flicker of "awareness." And that all their operations are driven by mathematics and not conscious thought. And that they are trained to mimic and simulate human communication so as to give the illusion of personal interaction.

So, when exactly do they become "conscious?" Is it when they are infused with a critical mass of data? Or when they are trained on the simulation of complex cognitive capabilities?

We know that simply aggregating endless data and countless algorithms in a system cannot make it sentient. We know too that programming it to perform personalized engagement—no matter how complex—does not produce a mysterious transformation whereby (when the smoke clears) a conscious subject emerges. To believe otherwise is pure superstition based on zero evidence and the violation of what we know of scientific law.

According to the authors of "There is no such thing as conscious artificial intelligence," a paper in *Humanities and Social Sciences Communications* (a *Nature* journal), the idea of conscious AI is simply deeply flawed science fiction:

> "There is no such thing as conscious AI. We argue that the association between consciousness and the computer algorithms used today (primarily large language models, LLMs), as well as those that would be invented in the foreseeable future, is deeply flawed. We believe that these flawed associations arise from a lack of technical knowledge and the way several new technologies (especially LLMs) work, which can create the illusion of consciousness. Moreover, we argue that the public discourse about AI is skewed by "sci-fitisation", which involves the unsubstantiated influence of fictional content on perceptions of this technology. To justify our claim, we reveal the incoherence in the argument that several computer algorithms are treated differently from other computer algorithms despite congruent modes of operation and a reliance on binary code and semiconductors. We believe that mathematical algorithms implemented on graphics cards cannot become conscious because they lack a complex biological substrate. We emphasise that the recognition of the consciousness of LLMs on the basis of their assertions is flawed because the language usage of LLMs is strictly probabilistic. Unfortunately, because the remarkable linguistic abilities of LLMs are increasingly capable of misleading people, people may attribute imaginary qualities to LLMs. Thus, a socially dangerous phenomenon referred to as 'semantic pareidolia' is reinforcing."[54]

54 *Humanities and Social Sciences Communications*, A *Nature* journal, volume 12, Article number: 1647. https://www.nature.com/articles/s41599-025-05868-8

Zombies R Us—Normalizing Nonsense

"Are zombies possible? They're not just possible, they're actual. We're all zombies. Nobody is conscious—not in the systematically mysterious way that supports such doctrines as epiphenomenalism! I can't prove that no such sort of consciousness exists. I also cannot prove that gremlins don't exist. The best I can do is show that there is no respectable motivation for believing in it."[55]

—*Daniel Dennett, Consciousness Explained*

"For Dennett there is no difference between us humans and complex zombies who lack any inner feelings, because we are all just complex zombies. … I regard his view as self-refuting because it denies the existence of the data which a theory of consciousness is supposed to explain."[56]

—*John Searle*

"There is not the slightest reason to doubt that brains are anything other than machines... our minds are merely complex processes."

—*Marvin Minsky, 1980s*

"A person is a mind file. A person is a software program."

—*Ray Kurzweil*

"There is only one sort of sort of stuff, namely matter—the physical stuff of physics, chemistry and physiology—and the mind is somehow nothing but a physical phenomenon."[57]

—*Daniel Dennett, Consciousness Explained*

"Alas, his [Dennett's] story does not hold together. Some of the problems posed by mental phenomena Dennett simply dismisses without adequate reason; others he ignores. Most, however, he attempts to prove are mere "user-illusions" generated by evolutionary history,

55 (New York: Little, Brown and Company, 1991), 406.

56 https://www.nybooks.com/articles/1995/12/21/the-mystery-of-consciousness-an-exchange/

57 (New York: Little, Brown and Company, 1991), 33.

even though this sometimes involves claims so preposterous as to verge on the deranged. In every case, most of his argument consists in a small set of simple logical errors. … The attempt to reduce the phenomena of mental existence to a purely physical history has been attempted before, and has so far always failed."[58]

—*David Bentley Hart*

"Right on page one, these computer scientists and philosophers [the authors of the Butlin Report] set forth their guiding assumption: "We adopt computational functionalism, the thesis that performing computations of the right kind is necessary and sufficient for consciousness, as a working hypothesis." Computational functionalism takes as its starting point the idea that consciousness is essentially a kind of software running on the hardware of what could be a brain or a computer—the theory is completely agnostic. But is computational functionalism true? … Just about anyplace you push on it, the computer-as-brain metaphor breaks down. Computer scientists treat neurons in a brain as though they are transistors on a chip, switched on or off by pulses of electricity. That analogy has some truth to it, but it is complicated by the fact that electricity is not the only factor influencing the firing of neurons. Brains are also awash in chemicals, including neuromodulators and hormones that powerfully influence the behavior of neurons, not just whether or not they fire but how strongly. … To liken neurons to transistors is to grossly underestimate their complexity. Compared with transistors on a chip, neurons in the brain are massively interconnected, each one communicating directly with as many as 10,000 others in a network so intricate that we are still decades away from being able to draw even the crudest map of its connections. In computer science, much has been made about the advent of "deep artificial neural networks"—a type of machine-learning architecture, supposedly modeled on the brain's, that layers a mind-boggling number of processors in such a way that the network can process and learn from vast troves of data. Impressive, for sure, yet a recent study demonstrated that a single cortical neuron can do everything an entire deep artificial neural network can."[59]

—*Michael Pollan, A World Appears: A Journey into Consciousness*

"Despite the vast number of facts being accumulated, our understanding of the brain appears to be approaching an impasse. In

58 https://www.thenewatlantis.com/publications/the-illusionist

59 (New York: Penguin Press. 2026), 102,104.

reality, the very structures of a brain and a computer are completely different. ...

A neuron is not like a binary switch that can be turned on or off, forming a wiring diagram. Instead, neurons respond in an analogue way, changing their activity in response to changes in stimulation. The nervous system alters its working by changes in the patterns of activation in networks of cells composed of large numbers of units; it is these networks that channel, shift and shunt activity. Unlike any device we have yet envisaged, the nodes of these networks are not stable points like transistors or valves, but sets of neurons—hundreds, thousands, tens of thousands strong—that can respond consistently as a network over time, even if the component cells show inconsistent behaviour. Understanding even the simplest of such networks is currently beyond our grasp."[60]

—*Matthew Cobb, The Idea of the Brain*

"Neuroscience does not address, let alone answer, the fundamental question of the relation(s) between matter and mind, body and mind, or brain and mind. If it seems to do so this is only a result of confusion between three quite different relations: correlation, causation and identity."[61]

—*Clinical neurologist Raymond Tallis*

"If you want to know about the mind, study the mind—not the brain, and certainly not the genes."[62]

—*Jerry Fodor*

"It is the animal that perceives, not parts of its brain, and it is human beings who think and reason, not their brains. The brain and its activities *make it possible* for *us*—not for *it*—to perceive and think, to feel emotions, and to form and pursue projects.

By speaking of the brain thinking and reasoning, about one hemisphere knowing something and not informing the other, about the brain making decisions without the person knowing, ... and so forth, neuroscientists are fostering a form of mystification and cultivating a

60 https://www.theguardian.com/science/2020/feb/27/why-your-brain-is-not-a-computer-neuroscience-neural-networks-consciousness

61 Raymond Tallis, *Aping Mankind* (Durham, UK: Acumen, 2011), 85.

62 *Times Literary Supplement*, 16 May 2003, 1–2.

neuro-mythology that are altogether deplorable."[63]

—*M.R. Bennett (former President of the International Society for Autonomic Neuroscience) and P.M.S. Hacker (Wittgensteinian philosopher of mind), Philosophical Foundations of Neuroscience*

MATCHING THE MOVEMENT to personalize computers is a movement to computerize persons.

Many practitioners of the digital dark arts assume that mind is a matter of matter. For this we have the philosophers to thank. And the occasional neuroscientist. A Frankenstein feedback loop.

There's much to be said about all this but let's begin with a comedy routine.

"After more than a century of looking for it, brain researchers have long since concluded that there is no conceivable place for such a self to be located in the physical brain, and that it simply doesn't exist,"[64] proclaims *Time*. "Science of the Soul? 'I Think, Therefore I Am' Is Losing Force"[65] notes the *New York Times*.

According to the neuroscientist V.S. Ramachandran,

> "All the richness of our mental life—our religious sentiments and even what each of us regards as his own intimate private self—is simply the activity of these little specks of jelly in your head, in your brain. There is nothing else." In an interview, Ramachandran goes on to say that "the soul as it is usually spoken of, namely an immaterial spirit that occupies individual brains and that only evolved in humans—all that is complete nonsense." Belief in that kind of soul "is basically superstition," he said.[66]

63 (Oxford: Blackwell Publishing, 2003), 3, 409.

64 Michael Lemonick, "Glimpses of the Brain," *Time*, July 17, 1995, 52.

65 Cornelia Dean in the *New York Times*, June 26, 2007, http://www.nytimes.com/2007/06/26/science/26soul.html?_r=1&ref=science

66 BBC Reith Lectures, ww.bbc.co.uk/radio4/reith2003. *New York Times*, June 26, 2007.

What makes this a comedy routine is the stunning incongruity between WHAT is being said and THAT it is being said.

> Speaking as one blob of jelly to another, let "me" assure "you" that "you" and "I" are simply blobs of jelly and that "my" argument itself is just the behavior of billions of nerve cells.

Truth be told, there is no truth.

> There are neurons and synapses, amygdalas and prefrontal cortexes. But no "you" or "me" in between or above or inside these — that would be to introduce the "ghost" of the dreaded Descartes or "a spiritual force" or the "superstition" of an "immaterial spirit."

"We" are not having this conversation. All that can be said is that two groups of neural networks and vocal cords are emitting vibes of various kinds.

> There can be no "understanding" because that would mean encoding and decoding symbols and discerning meaning and such activities would require an understander.

"You" and "I" cannot possibly exist or be conscious because there are no properties of self-hood and consciousness in the "vast assembly of nerve cells"; and since there is continuous change in the molecules making up these cells there is nothing there that can sustain identity or continuity.

> The neural activities simply drive themselves since there is no "one" to drive them. Bottom-line: there's nothing but molecules in motion.

It is paradoxical indeed that some of the very professionals who study mental functions promote a view that (coming from any other source) would be classified as a mental disorder.

In good time, we will drill deeper into the roots of these self-refuting ideas.

As a preview, we can say that famous modern philosophers have said without embarrassment that consciousness doesn't exist, that we don't have beliefs or desires or intentions and that we don't exist. In denying what is self-evident, they haven't given arguments but used metaphors and so-called thought-experiments and issued dark warnings about threats to their Victorian-era paradigm of science.

Why do some intellectuals countenance such absurd views? George Orwell's comment is appropriate here: "One has to belong to the intelligentsia to believe things like that. No ordinary man could be such a fool."[67]

To what end? The science of the late 19th century considered itself complete. But two discrepancies in the establishment narratives exploded into the revolutions of relativity and quantum mechanics that changed the entire paradigm of modern science.

A parallel situation exists today as upholders of the *ancien regime* try to maintain the fiction that matter is all that matters. But each new dyke erected to uphold status quo dogmas has been washed away by floods of new evidence. The establishment view has to be constantly revised.

The dance routines adopted in this game of musical chairs reflect the desperation of the relevant ideologues. From the belly dance of Behaviorism we moved to the breakdance headspin of Eliminative Materialism, the twist of the Identity Theorists, the tap dance of the Functionalists, the ballet of the non-reductive Materialists, the walz of the Anomalous Monists, the mime dance of the Epiphenomenalists and the folk dance of the Emergentists.

But it was all to no avail. Every escape-route from consciousness, thought and the self ended up as a dead-end.

The root of all this confusion can be traced not just to the mind-is-matter school but also to the Cartesian dualists. Both these equal and

67 George Orwell, *Notes on Nationalism*, May, 1945. http://www.resort.com/~prime8/Orwell/nationalism.html

opposite views have split the unified human agent into a multiplicity of random parts. As we will soon see, the only account of human bodily, sensory and cognitional experience that works is Aristotelian holism.

Algorithmic Animism

THE HYPNOTIC HOLD of the idea of thinking, conscious AI derives from an ancient pathology of the human psyche—animism.

Animism, said the 19th century anthropologist E.B. Tylor, is "the animation of all nature,"[68] a widely held belief in primitive societies. For the animists, said J.G. Frazier in *The Golden Bough*, there were spirits in "every tree and flower, brook and river, every breeze that blew and every cloud that flecked with silvery white the blue expanse of heaven."[69] Said Tylor, animists had "a sense of spiritual beings…inhabiting trees and rocks and waterfalls."

Animism was the personification of all the activity evident in nature. Later science gave a more accurate—if less dramatic—explanation for such activity, the laws of nature. Lightning issues forth from electrical discharges in the atmosphere not the wrath of the spirits.

Today there is a New Animism, one that has captured the imagination of the AI universe. You might call it Algorithmic Animism. Just as we once personalized rivers and trees, we now personalize chatbots and computing systems.

If you throw together enough data and sprinkle an ensemble of algorithms into the brew, then "a miracle happens." Strange things happen when black boxes reach a tipping point. Complexity works its own magic. And a star is born. Or, from a sociological standpoint, a religion.

68 Tylor, E. B., *Primitive Culture: Researches into the Development of Mythology, Philosophy, Religion, Language, Art and Custom*, Vol. 1 (London: John Murray, 1929).

69 Geoffrey Parrinder, *World Religions* (New York: Facts on File, 1985), 32.

The New Animism is built on the same mind-set as the older version. You can't see the spirit but there's enough activity to warrant our belief that there's someone like us behind the scenes.

We may argue that mere bits and bytes and mathematical manipulations cannot produce intelligence and intentionality. But when a machine shows seemingly intelligent and intentional behavior, it seems plausible to attribute these to a "spirit" or, in today's parlance, a consciousness.

The primordial revelation behind the new religion is the Turing Test. If a computer's intelligent behavior can't be distinguished from a human's, then, for all practical purposes, it has a mind.

But, as we have seen, this primordial revelation is simply a demonstrably false dogma. A sophisticated calculator can perform computations that go beyond the capabilities of most humans—but no one concludes from this that the calculator has a mind. More to the point, as Christopher Mims describes it, the Turing Test has become the Turing Trap:

> "Rather than demonstrating that machines have achieved intelligence, the Turing Test shows that linguistic fluency is possible even in its absence."

Like the old animists, the New Animists invoke non-physical forces to explain physical phenomena without any supporting evidence. At least the old animism went away with the discovery of the laws of nature.

But the New Animists have no such excuse. From the start they knew that the generative AIs are purely mathematical artifacts. And yet they invoke new mystical forces to explain behavior that they know is entirely embedded in the software and hardware they created themselves.

Amusingly, Algorithmic Animists often also profess the Zombies 'R Us creed. When human agents manifest attributes that are experienced as immaterial, these dimensions are simply ignored.

But the abilities of being aware, of processing concepts that have no physical locus and of maintaining self-identity despite ceaseless molecular change cannot be denied. They demand an explanation.

Genesis of an Illusion—The "Information Processing Language Game"

"The computational theory of mind is the most impressive illustration of the power of thinking by transferred epithet: how, by shuttling between machines (in this case computers), brains, and minds, the same terms can straddle the mind-brain barrier and make the idea that mind or consciousness is made of nerve impulses almost impossible to question. A picture holds us captive and we can't get out of it because it lies in our language.

So what is the computational theory of mind? At its heart is the assumption that *the mind is to the brain what software is to hardware*. To put it slightly differently, the mind is a set of computer programs implemented in the wetware of the brain. Allied to this is the key idea ... that the essential business of mind is to *process information* and that processing information is (also) what the brain does. ... By virtue of the suggestion that it is a cluster of naturally evolved computers, the mind is both naturalized and computerized. ...

It is the assumption that what brains, conscious and unconscious minds and computers do, above all, is to acquire, process, store and transmit information that seems to provide the most powerful justification for describing the mind in terms of the computational activity of the brain. ...

The extended misuse of the term 'information' is absolutely pivotal to establishing the conceptual confusions necessary to the seeming fruitfulness and apparent explanatory power of much modern thought about the brain and the mind—and ourselves. This converges in the computational theory of mind. By playing on different meanings of 'information' and transferring epithets like a volleyball, it is possible to argue that minds, brains, organisms, various artefacts such as computers, and even non-living thermodynamic systems are all information-processing devices. …

Once the concept of information is liberated from the idea of *a conscious someone being informed* and from that of *a conscious someone doing the informing*, anything is possible. Language bewitches us and we imagine that the problem of consciousness has been solved when in fact it has simply been concealed by verbal legerdemain."[70]

—*Raymond Tallis*

"The computational model is implausible as an account of global cognition. … The more global … a cognitive process the less anyone understands it. … If someone were to ask us why we should even suppose that the digital computer is even a plausible mechanism for the simulation of global cognitive processes, the answering silence would be deafening."[71]

—*Jerry Fodor, pioneer of the computational theory of mind*

"No matter how hard they try, brain scientists and cognitive psychologists will never find a copy of Beethoven's 5th Symphony in the brain—or copies of words, pictures, grammatical rules or any other kinds of environmental stimuli. …

Our shoddy thinking about the brain has deep historical roots, but the invention of computers in the 1940s got us especially confused. For more than half a century now, psychologists, linguists, neuroscientists and other experts on human behaviour have been asserting that the human brain works like a computer. …

Senses, reflexes and learning mechanisms—this is what we start with, and it is quite a lot, when you think about it. If we lacked any of these capabilities at birth, we would probably have trouble surviving. But here is what we are *not* born with: *information, data, rules, software, knowledge, lexicons, representations, algorithms, programs, models, memories, images, processors, subroutines, encoders, decoders, symbols, or buffers*—design elements that allow digital computers to behave somewhat intelligently. Not only are we not *born* with such things, we also don't *develop* them—ever.

70 Raymond Tallis, *Aping Mankind* (Durham, UK: Acumen, 2011), 194, 199, 208.

71 Jerry Fodor, *The Modularity of Mind: An Essay in Faculty Psychology* (Cambridge, MA: MIT Press 1983), 107, 129.

We don't *store* words or the rules that tell us how to manipulate them. We don't create *representations* of visual stimuli, *store* them in a short-term memory buffer, and then *transfer* the representation into a long-term memory device. We don't *retrieve* information or images or words from memory registers. Computers do all of these things, but organisms do not. …

Computers really do operate on *symbolic representations* of the world. They really *store* and *retrieve*. They really *process*. They really have physical *memories*. They really are guided in everything they do, without exception, by *algorithms*.

Humans, on the other hand, do not—never did, never will. Given this reality, why do so many scientists talk about our mental life as if we were computers? …

We are organisms, not computers. *Get over it.* Let's get on with the business of trying to understand ourselves, but without being encumbered by unnecessary intellectual baggage. The IP metaphor has had a half-century run, producing few, if any, insights along the way. The time has come to hit the DELETE key."[72]

—Robert Epstein, former editor-in-chief of Psychology Today and founder, American Institute for Behavioral Research and Technology.

"Information has been used to explain mental representation. … Although there are some advantages of this approach, mental representation cannot be reduced to informational processes for two reasons. First, informational processes cannot cover the distinctively subjective feature of mental representation, Second, informational processes cannot characterize the semantic properties of mental representation."[73]

—Wei Jiang, "Information and Mental Representation"

"To insist on trying to explain the mind in terms of concepts and theories that have been devised exclusively to explain nonmental phenomena is, in view of the radically distinguishing characteristics of the mental, both intellectually backward and scientifically suicidal."[74]

—Thomas Nagel, The View from Nowhere

72 https://aeon.co/essays/your-brain-does-not-process-information-and-it-is-not-a-computer

73 https://www.mdpi.com/2504-3900/47/1/51

74 (Oxford: Oxford University Press, 1986), 52.

> "Consider for example the proceedings that we call "games." I mean board-games, card-games, ball-games, Olympic games, and so on. What is common to them all? Don't say: "There must be something common, or they would not be called 'games' but look and see whether there is anything common to all. For if you look at them you will not see something that is common to all, but similarities, relationships, and a whole series of them at that. Look for example at board-games, with their multifarious relationships. Now pass to card-games; here you find many correspondences with the first group, but many common features drop out, and others appear. When we pass next to ball- games, much that is common is retained, but much is lost. … Is there always winning and losing, or competition between players? Think of patience [Solitaire]. In ball games there is winning and losing; but when a child throws his ball at the wall and catches it again, this feature has disappeared. Look at the parts played by skill and luck; and at the difference between skill in chess and skill in tennis. Think now of games like ring-a-ring-a-roses; here is the element of amusement, but how many other characteristic features have disappeared! And we can go through the many, many other groups of games in the same way; can see how similarities crop up and disappear."[75]
>
> —*Ludwig Wittgenstein, Philosophical Investigations*

THE TWO TRENDS of normalizing nonsense and algorithmic animism became a perfect storm with the introduction of "information processing" as the governing metaphor of science, technology and even philosophy.

The notion of "information processing" has created a metaphoric morass in which a menagerie of unrelated activities are identified with each other. Apples and oranges, stars and butterflies, computers and humans and everything else that exists are viewed as manifestations of a single activity—information processing.

75 Translated by G.E.M. Anscombe (Oxford, UK: Basil Blackwell, 1958), 66.

Thus, the interaction of quantum fields; DNA synthesis; cellular signaling; sensory perception, i.e., the conversion of physical and chemical stimuli into electrical energy transmitted via charged ions; software systems, i.e., human commands translated into electrical signals (via operating systems, etc.) then converted to machine code to switch on transistors and other components; AI, i.e., applying math to respond to queries and commands by quantifying and classifying bodies of data; human thought, i.e., subjective analysis and synthesis using immaterial concepts by a person; are all presented as modes of "information processing," different in degree but not in kind.

The consequence of this madcap blurring of boundaries is the mayhem we find in contemporary discussions of AI language models and human thought.

Ludwig Wittgenstein's analogy of language-games pinpoints the flaw permeating all levels of this trainwreck of thought.

Wittgenstein draws an analogy between different games and the different fields of knowledge. We play different games: tennis, marbles, billiards, football, basketball. The concepts in these games often differ radically. A "foul" in basketball makes no sense in tennis, a good move in chess is meaningless in a game of marbles. There is no rule, which can be applied in every game: the "rules" of one game are not rules in another and often do not make sense in the other. Even the word "game" cannot be said to have one meaning for it means entirely different things in different games.

When we apply the language-game analogy to "information processing," we find that neither information nor processing are used in identical or even similar senses across various domains.

Information theory is foundational to AI. It is the bridge between data and mathematical decision-making. But "information" in information theory has no bearing on information as normally understood. It refers to reducing uncertainty when an event takes place. It is a mathematical concept not a semantic one. According to one of its pioneers, Warren Weaver, "Information in the theory is used in a special sense that must not be confused with ordinary usage. In particular, information must not be confused with meaning. In fact, two messages one of which is heavily loaded with meaning and the other of which is pure nonsense, can be exactly equivalent, from the present viewpoint, as regards information."[76]

DNA contains information in the sense that its chemical bases provide instruction sets for the cell's molecular machinery for it to be transcribed into RNA and then translated into amino acids linked so as to build proteins.

Quantum fields contain information in the sense of containing their fundamental physical properties such as mass, charge, spin and momentum.

Information in each of these instances means something entirely different. They are as different in nature as water polo, ping pong and bridge.

What is more, none of them refer to information in the normal sense of data that are meaningful to a recipient. To create and grasp meaning, you need a human subject who is conscious and capable of conceptual thought.

> "Information processing" in the truest sense is "semantic processing," understanding the meaning of data. And that requires a human person with an intellect.

As we will see down the road, broadbrush applications of the "information processing" model led to fallacious ideas of syntactic engines and semantic engines.

76 Warren Weaver, "Recent contributions to the Mathematical Theory of Communications."

The table below illustrates the contrast between different kinds of "information" and "processing":

Source	Recipient	Information	"Processing"	Conscious awareness?	Conscious Understanding?
Laws of nature	Mass/ energy	Quantum mechanics, relativity, thermodynamics	Interaction of particles, fields	No	No
Genetic code	Autonomous agents (living beings)	Stored in DNA and RNA	Proteins built using transcription and translation	No	No
Sensory receptors	Neurons	Receive, process, transmit inputs	Electro-chemical	No	No
Software programs, AI	Hardware	Instructions resulting in actions performed for user	Electrical pulses	No	No
Human self	Intellect	Grasp meaning from data	Immaterial concepts formed from percepts and used in analysis and communications	Yes	Yes

In considering information processing, the distinctions become clear when we ask the questions of Who, How and Why. In actual information processing, the "Who" is a conscious agent, the "How" is perceptual or conceptual thought and the "Why" is purpose and reason.

Non-human animals are conscious and capable of perceptual thought. Humans are unique for their capabilities of conceptual thought (meaning-processing) and self-consciousness.

There is an essential pre-condition for information processing by a human mind: that it is conscious (subjectivity) and capable of perceiving meaning (semantics). The assumption of most computational theories of mind is that what we are talking about is the brain applying computational processes like algorithms to representational structures encoded in it; hence, information processing.

But it is impossible to conceive of representational structures or models that are entirely physical in nature. Representing or visualizing something has a conscious, non-physical dimension albeit integrated with physical processes. And representing by its nature suggests that it is meaningful.

Wei Jiang highlights the obvious:

> Can information cover the mentality of mental representation? There are a lot of things in the world carrying information, but they are not mental representations. For instance, smoke might imply fire, thermometers signify the temperature of the surroundings, and computers store a lot of information and function in terms of the computation of information. However, none of them are mental representations. For a state to be mental representation, there must be something distinctive that makes it mental rather than non-mental. ... There are two features of mental representation that make it special. First, mental representation is subjective ... Second, mental representation has been considered as having semantic properties."

Colin McGinn shows why consciousness is fundamental:

> According to the Representational Theory of Mind, "the mind is a device for representing things—that is its essence. Hence, the computational theory of mind. But where is consciousness in all this? It seems irrelevant, since the mental language is deemed unconscious. ... The mind, thus conceived, could be completely unconscious and still be the mind. There is nothing particularly *conscious* about the mind. Behaviorism ignored consciousness in favor of bodily behavior; representationalism ignores it too. The representations are internal, to be sure, but they have nothing intrinsically to do with consciousness. But doesn't that sound wrong? Isn't the mind that we all have a conscious mind (though we have an unconscious

> mind too)? You can't subtract consciousness from the story and do justice to mind as it actually exists; thought itself frequently comes to us clothed in consciousness. Accordingly, RTM is a false theory."[77]

For true information processing there has to be a "who" that does the processing, a conscious, cogitative state that is the "how" of the processing and the intending/understanding that is the "why" of the processing.

77 https://colinmcginn.net/consciousness-and-mental-representation/

Superstitions

"It has often been said, and certainly not without justification, that the man of science is a poor philosopher."[78]

—*Albert Einstein, Out of My Later Years*

"There's no opinion so absurd but that a philosopher hasn't expressed it."

—*Cicero*

"There is only one thing a philosopher can be relied upon to do, and that is to contradict other philosophers."

—*William James*

Physicalist theories belong to "the numerous class of theories which are so preposterously silly that only very learned men could have thought of them. But such theories are frequently countenanced by the naive since they are put forward in highly technical terms by learned persons who are themselves too confused to know exactly what they mean."[79]

—*C.D. Broad, The Mind and Its Place in Nature*

THUS FAR, for the most part, we have been studying the "machines have minds" spell cast by the AIs of our age.

Inevitably, there is some overlap with the older "humans have no minds" spell.

With good reason, we can say that some of the best minds of modern times have lost their minds. This is by their own admission!

78 (New York: Philosophical Library, 1950), 58.

79 (London: Kegan Paul, 1925), 623.

The two spells in tandem have spawned a super-set of superstitions to which all intellectuals in good standing must pledge allegiance:

> I am not conscious
>
> There is no "I"
>
> There are no such things as beliefs or desires: the idea that these are real is unscientific "folk psychology": all we have are physical neuronal transactions
>
> We are not capable of intentions or purposes since we are limited to physical processes
>
> Likewise, we do not act on the basis of reasons because the only factors at work are physical causes
>
> All our thinking is simply and solely the firing of neurons
>
> We cannot "mean" anything since our brains are driven by impersonal forces and "meaning" is not something that can be physically quantified
>
> We are (stochastic) parrots because, like an AI, we are not capable of actually understanding anything but operate by matching patterns and making predictions using statistics and probability
>
> We cannot choose or decide: all our actions are the product of physical and environmental causes
>
> We can download our minds on a hard drive (or some such device) and thus make multiple copies of ourselves

To break the two spells and restore our sanity, we have to shake off these superstitions. This means opening our eyes to what is obvious.

Hard Facts

"The average neuron, consisting of about 100,000 molecules, is about 80% water. The brain is home to about 100 billion such cells and thus about 1015 molecules. Each neuron gets 10,000 or so connections from other cells in the brain. Within each neuron, the molecules are replaced approximately 10,000 times in an average life span. Yet humans have a continuous sense of self that is stable over time."[80]

—*Neuroscientist Mario Beauregard*

"None of these people [with various brain disorders including degenerative conditions such as Alzheimer's] lose their entire sense of self through the loss of any one cognitive module. They still have a first-person perspective on the fact that they are a person with a sense of self."[81]

—*Masud Husain, Professor of Cognitive Neuroscience, Oxford University, "The Neuroscience of the Self"*

So here's what's obvious.

We are conscious and conscious that we are conscious. Our conscious experience includes sensations, memories, images, concepts, intentions and choices.

In terms of how we experience them, conscious phenomena are different in kind from anything physical, anything that can be physically observed, described or quantified. Sensations and perceptions have no size or shape, no physical characteristics whatsoever.

80 Mario Beauregard (and Denyse O'Leary), *The Spiritual Brain* (New York: Harper One, 2007), 114.

81 https://time.com/article/2026/04/15/the-neuroscience-of-the-self/

In terms of scientific investigation, it is clear that there is nothing in the brain that has any property of consciousness. Consciousness cannot even be described in scientific terms.

We are capable of discerning meaning as demonstrated most clearly in our use of language whereby we process semantic symbols and use syntactical rules effortlessly—and in our reading and understanding this sentence.

We instinctively create and grasp concepts. Our senses make us aware of the physical world. We then process what we perceive, the "percepts," to produce a concept. A concept is something that does not refer to a specific physical thing or being. From the animals we encounter, we understand the concept of "animal", something that is not a specific animal. We are exercised by ideals of liberty and justice. These have no physical counterpart. Sensations and perceptions are triggered by physical objects. But thoughts involving concepts are not driven by the physical (although we can use physical media like writing and speaking). And it makes no sense to talk of storing immaterial concepts in the brain, a material organ.

We see things from a first-person perspective (I, me, my, mine). The "first-person" is not something that can be included in any physical or scientific description of the world.

We have a unifying center of our biological life, our consciousness and our intellectual operations, an author of our experiences and actions, that we might call the self. We are "mind-full" organisms with a unifying intellectual, sensory self.

We maintain our continued self-identity over the course of our lives, although the molecules in our neurons change thousands of times across a lifetime.

> We are capable of intending and choosing and executing our intentions and choices and most of our actions can only be understood as the result of intentions and choices.
>
> Our thoughts and intentions have a "life" of their own and our processes of reasoning or deciding proceed on their own dynamic. These thoughts and intentions are accompanied by neural activity but there is no question that it is the thoughts and intentions that drive the transactions in the brain and not the other way round.

Especially compelling is the inescapable fact highlighted by Beauregard that dooms the mind-is-matter superstition.

Your brain is made up of some 80+ billion neurons. Each neuron is made up of an average of some 100,000 molecules. These molecules change thousands of times over the course of your life. And yet you remain the same at two months old, two years old, 20 years old and all the way to now.

Of course, you grow and learn and change but it is the same "you" that undergoes these changes.

So, what is it that stays the same? It is clearly not something physical because the physical—for instance, your neurons—is in a constant state of molecular flux. You could not even complete a sentence if you were entirely physical.

And all the cells in your body are constantly dying and being replenished, so they cannot serve as the basis of a continuing identity.

Indubitably, then, there is something about you that is immaterial, non-physical.

Did the brain produce this non-physical dimension?

No, because the laws of physics have no room for the creation of the non-physical from the physical.

But there's even more to consider.

We are not talking here about hypotheses or inferences. When we say we are conscious or capable of using concepts, we are not trying to explain the data of our immediate experience.

On the contrary, these are themselves the immediate data of our experience.

In other words, our consciousness (awareness) of our environment, our capability of intellectual understanding especially as manifested in language and our unified first person self-identity are the raw data.

They are self-evident and self-authenticating.

So where does that leave the "other side?"

Let the games begin.

II

"TO THINE OWN SELF BE TRUE"

HAMLET, ACT 1, SCENE 3

> "The late philosopher Morris R. Cohen of CCNY was asked by a student in the metaphysics course, Professor Cohen, how do I know that I exist? The keen old prof replied, And who is asking?"
>
> —*Saul Bellow, Humboldt's Gift.*

> "I accept the great adventure of being me."
>
> —*Simone de Beauvoir, Notebooks for a Youth*

"THAT WAY MADNESS LIES"[82]

FROM THE CLAIM THAT AIs can think and feel, we turn to humans. Do we think and feel and who are "we"? And how does this tie into what we know of the world?

We encountered the view that we are our brains. All mental-speak is brain-speak. Nothing more.

But we have also seen that we somehow maintain our self-identity despite the constant change in our neuronal make-up. How is it possible for us to stay the same—or make it through this sentence— if we are entirely molecules in motion?

So, there's nothing open-and-shut about the mind-as-physical argument. In fact, the shoe is on the other foot.

The "I" that I am seems not to be entirely physical.

---

82 *King Lear*, Act 3, Scene 4

Of course, this view has been fiercely rejected, resisted and ridiculed by the intellectual trend-setters of our time.

And yet our everyday experience of consciousness, thought and our selves seems to be undeniable.

Yes, we are physical beings. But these three human "powers" have no physical properties—although they are integrated with the physical. They cannot be quantified in physical terms or derived from a material matrix.

What are we missing?

Do the cognoscenti know something that is opaque to the rest of us rubes?

It was the contention of the previous section that consciousness, conceptual thought and the self are "hard facts" that are self-evident and self-authenticating.

They are the data from which we start. They are not hypotheses that need to be proven. Admittedly, not everyone believes this to be the case. The physicalists—those who believe that only the physical exists—dismiss the three as illusions.

But denial of the self-evident results in self-contradiction. Are you conscious of the fact that consciousness is an illusion? Isn't "illusion" a concept and therefore an example of conceptual thought? And if it's all an illusion, who is having the illusion?

There is also the question of sanity. Can you survive, let alone live in society, if you act as if the three are illusory?

Also, when I say, "I feel a sharp pain in my lower back," the sensation in question is not something that can be demonstrated or disproven. Likewise with my claim to be thinking about a theorem or reflecting on my life over the last year. But the fact that I cannot "prove" these "encounters" does not by any means imply that they are not real.

The whole problem with physicalism is the refusal to start with what is obvious in our immediate experience. It is a problem that has a long history in philosophy.

Descartes needed to infer his existence from the fact that he was thinking instead of starting with the fact of his existence (which could not be denied without self-contradiction). The same pattern of denying the undeniable is found in David Hume, Immanuel Kant and myriad other philosophers.

But there is no reason for us to follow in their self-defeating footsteps. Life's too short!

We will, nevertheless, make the case here for the reality of consciousness, conceptual thought and the intellectual self—if only to celebrate their wonder and power.

Following that, in the next section, we will address the challenges posed by the physicalists.

The question before those pursuing this inquiry is not one of "there are two sides to every issue." Rather, on the one hand, we have "hard facts" of immediate experience that can only be denied on pain of self-contradiction and absurdity. On the other, we have the denial of these hard facts and a perpetual recycling of doomed "square the circle" arguments.

But there is no obligation for us to sink into the quicksand created by the "madding crowd" of deniers. As King Lear warned, "That way madness lies; let me shun that; No more of that."

"NOW IS THE WINTER OF OUR DISCONTENT MADE GLORIOUS SUMMER"[83]

There are, however, some hopeful signs on the horizon.

Yes, the nature of consciousness, thought and the self was ignored, dismissed or explained away by many—but not all—scientists and philosophers for well over a hundred years.

That was because many of these thinkers felt more at home with physicalism, alternatively described as materialism. In their view, all of reality was reducible to the physical.

Yet a cascade of radical developments has eviscerated the seemingly unassailable foundations of physicalism.

Among philosophers, the publication of *The Waning of Materialism* by Oxford University Press, with contributions from over 20 prominent philosophers, was a major milestone. In the introduction to the book, we read that an approximate majority of influential philosophers active over the last sixty years have rejected materialism:

> "Materialism is waning in a number of significant respects—one of which is the ever-growing number of major philosophers who reject materialism or at least have strong sympathies with anti-materialist views. It is of course commonly thought that over the course of the last sixty or so years of materialism achieved hegemony in academic philosophy, and this is no doubt right by certain measures ... It is therefore surprising that an examination of the major philosophers active in this period reveals that a majority, or something approaching a majority, either rejected materialism or had serious and specific doubts about its ultimate viability. ... Materialism plainly has not achieved hegemony when it comes to philosophers of this high caliber.
>
> Historically, materialism was just the reductionist position that

83 *Richard III*, Act 1, Scene 1

> mental properties are identical to—and in that sense are nothing but—physical properties.
>
> Over the last fifty or so years, materialism has been challenged by a daunting list of arguments …Taken together, these arguments and sophisticated variations on them constitute a significant prima facie threat to the success of materialism. …
>
> As things stand today, materialism is at least on the defensive. In this respect, materialism is on the wane. This seems to be reflected in the attitudes of many contemporary philosophers of mind. A growing number—among them prominent philosophers who once had strong materialist sympathies—have come to the conclusion that at least some of the arguments against materialism cannot be overcome."[84]

Among scientists, the ferment in consciousness studies has led even some naturalists to admit that consciousness is a property as fundamental as matter.

Others admit that the nature and origin of language cannot be explained in the older behaviorist and computer models of the brain.

Very significantly, Christoph Koch, the scientist who launched the scientific study of consciousness in partnership with the Nobel Prize winner Francis Crick, has now abandoned physicalism.

As reported by Michael Pollan,

> Koch had gone through an experience that told him consciousness existed beyond the brain. Koch had long been the quintessential brain guy, going back to his early work with Crick. … For years, Koch, like just about everyone in the field, had taken it for granted that brains generate consciousness—*somehow*. … For like any other respectable scientist, he was a confirmed materialist. …

84 Robert C. Koons and George Bealer ed. *The Waning of Materialism* (New York: Oxford University Press, 2010), ix, x, xvii-xxi.

> It is significant for the field, I think, that a scientist of Koch's standing has come to doubt that scientific materialism (or physicalism, as it's sometimes called by scientists) will ever be able to explain consciousness. …
>
> When I asked him in a follow-up email to account for the change, he wrote this: 'I've certainly moved beyond garden-variety physicalism, for three reasons. First, the abject inability of physicalism to explain or even deal with consciousness.' For Koch that failure was exemplified by the move on the part of die-hard physicalists like Daniel Dennett 'to simply deny its existence and call it an illusion.' But to call consciousness an illusion makes no sense, Koch pointed out, for what is an illusion but a conscious experience? The other physicalist Hail Mary is to describe consciousness as an 'emergent property' of matter—neurons somehow properly arranged—but no one has yet specified how or why that might actually happen, making emergence sound less like a scientific explanation than an abracadabra. …
>
> Not everyone in the field has given up on finding a material explanation for consciousness. … Yet their theories require some hand-waving or brute force to bridge the gap between the operations of our brains and our subjective experiences. It does seem like the materialist approach to the hard problem of consciousness has hit a wall. …
>
> For most areas of scientific research, materialism 'works' just fine—until, that is, you get to the two metaphysical deal-breakers: quantum physics and consciousness science. Raising these doubts about materialism could turn out to be the most important legacy of the work done on consciousness since the early 1990's."[85]

Despite this monumental shift away from physicalism, many working scientists and philosophers continue to unreflectively wander in the FundaMaterialist wilderness. Those who cling to older paradigms find it hard to let go.

85 Michael Pollan, *A World Appears: A Journey into Consciousness* (New York: Penguin Press. 2026), 218-220.

A more productive approach for serious inquirers is to return to the data of our immediate experience. Accordingly, let us explore me and my self and my powers of awareness and intellection.

Regaining Consciousness

"There's a great deal of debate about how to define consciousness, but we are essentially talking about the thing that flickers to life when you wake up in the morning. But as far as understanding why it happens, I don't know that we're much closer than we've ever been. It's different from other scientific conundrums in that what we're asking is, how do you take physical pieces and parts and translate that into private, subjective experience, like the redness of red, or the pain of pain or the smell of cinnamon? And so not only do we not have a theory, but we don't really know what such a theory would look like that would explain our experience in physical or mathematical terms."[86]

—*Neuroscientist David Eagleman, author of The Brain*

Sensory consciousness first appeared several hundred million years ago. "A number of biologists and philosophers have argued that consciousness was born from a specific event in our evolutionary history: the Cambrian explosion. … For around 100 million years, from about 635 to 542 million years ago, the first large multicellular organisms emerged on Earth. … Then, quite suddenly by geological standards, most of these creatures disappeared. Between 530 and 520 million years ago, they were replaced by a remarkable proliferation of animals who lived quite differently. These animals started to move, to have brains and eyes, to seek out prey and avoid predators. … But they included the ancestors of all current species of animals, from insects, crustaceans and mollusks to the earliest vertebrates, the creatures who eventually turned into us. [Because of their new capabilities] they could learn about the world around them. These creatures developed the first simple brains, as well as new sensors like eyes and new tools like limbs and claws."[87]

—*Psychologist Alison Gopnik, "The Explosive Evolution of Consciousness"*

"Consciousness might feel like a transparent window on the world, but as we will discover, the world that appears to us is the product of

86 https://www.theguardian.com/science/2021/jun/12/david-eagleman-the-working-of-the-brain-resembles-drug-dealers-in-albuquerque

87 https://www.wsj.com/articles/the-explosive-evolution-of-consciousness-11559746175

consciousness; there's something out there, but since we have no way to access it—to perceive it, describe it, measure it, confirm its existence—*except* by way of consciousness, it is impossible to say what it is. … As much as scientists like to think they can achieve an objective third-person perspective on reality, they, too, know the world only through the scrim of consciousness—the tools of science and the choices of what to measure and how to measure it are all, inescapably, products of consciousness. The scientific enterprise is itself a specialized form of consciousness."[88]

—*Michael Pollan, A World Appears: A Journey into Consciousness*

"Consciousness pervades nearly all aspects of the human enterprise. Everything ever known or felt, seen, heard, believed, imagined, or experienced in any form has to be processed through this universal medium, the conscious mind. Conveyor of all our values, our sense of purpose and meaning, of right and wrong, of beauty, joy, and so on, consciousness is central to all that matters most in life. Any basic revision in its conception, therefore, or in its role, or how it relates to the physical brain or to outside reality is bound to produce sweeping reverberations."[89]

—*Nobel Prize winning neuroscientist Roger Sperry who led the consciousness revolution against Behaviorism*

"The case for concluding that consciousness is a metaphysically fundamental reality, not reducible to …any assembly of nonconscious physical things, is very strong. …

We cannot view from a standpoint outside our subjective experience the relation between consciousness and the nonconscious physical reality out of which it is assumed to arise and to which it is claimed to be reducible. No scientific experimentation or instrumentation can provide us with such a standpoint, for any standpoint must be taken from within consciousness. Thus no reductive effort, however, intensive or sophisticated, can be evaluated or understood apart from the essential involvement of the phenomenon it attempts to reduce….

To acknowledge the irreducible reality of consciousness with its intrinsic subjectivity should lead us … to acknowledge that there is a conscious subject at its center, in that it exists in virtue of its constitutive

88 Michael Pollan, op cit., xxvi

89 Roger W. Sperry, "A Search for Beliefs to Live by Consistent with Science" in Clifford N. Matthews and Roy Abraham Varghese, eds, *Cosmic Beginnings and Human Ends: Where Science and Religion Meet* (Chicago: Open Court, 1994), 315.

involvement in the states of the conscious subject or self whose consciousness it is."[90]

—*David Lund, The Conscious Self*

"The cerebellum is a denser structure than the cortex, with many more neurons, and yet it is generally considered not to be involved in the processes of consciousness. This enigma highlights the fact that no one can yet explain why the activity of one set of neurons produces consciousness, whereas that of another does not."[91]

—*Matthew Cobb, The Idea of the Brain: The Past and Future of Neuroscience*

"Given that there are so many popular articles about the brain lighting up during conscious activity, it is perhaps surprising that there are no consistent measures—neither EEG or fMRI—that can reliably distinguish conscious from unconscious individuals."[92]

—*Matthew Cobb, The Idea of the Brain: The Past and Future of Neuroscience*

"A dirty secret of modern science is that we have no way of explaining the fact that humans have conscious experience."[93]

—*Cognitive scientist Steven Pinker, "Deep Commonalities Between Life and Mind"*

"There is absolutely no basis for the assumption, central to Neuromania, that the intrinsically appearance-less material world will flower into appearance to a bit of that world (the brain) as a result of the particular material properties of that bit of the world: for instance, its ability to control the passage of sodium ions through semi-permeable membranes. We cannot expect to find anything in a material object, however fashioned, that can explain the difference between a thought and a pebble, or between a supposedly thoughtful brain and a definitely thoughtless kidney."[94]

—*Raymond Tallis, Aping Mankind*

"I now have difficulty even imagining anything scientific that would

---

90 David Lund, *The Conscious Self* (Buffalo New York: Prometheus Press, 2005), 385.

91 Matthew Cobb, *The Idea of the Brain: The Past and Future of Neuroscience* (New York: Basic Books, 2020), 352.

92 Ibid., 352.

93 Steven Pinker, "Deep Commonalities Between Life and Mind," in Alan Grafen and Mark Ridley. ed., *Richard Dawkins* (Oxford: Oxford University Press, 2006), 136.

94 Raymond Tallis, *Aping Mankind* (Durham, UK: Acumen, 2011), 143.

> explain the personal and subjective aspects of perception."[95]
>
> —*Neurophysiologist Horace Barlow in 2009 who had, in 1972, formulated his five dogmas of neuroscience which claimed to show how neural activity gives rise to subjective conscious experience.*

OUR FIRST STOP IS "consciousness" which is simply the power of being aware.

Let's take the phenomenon of seeing. How do we explain it? This is not a question of the origin of the eye.

Here is the central mystery in the phenomenon of physical vision: the fact that you and I can become directly and immediately aware of the world around us. Why is it the case that one piece of matter attains the capacity to become aware of another in so intimate and complete a fashion? Can anything in physical reality explain or even describe this ability to *be aware*? Viewed as a mode of awareness, the phenomenon of seeing is irreducible to anything physical or material.

Second, how and why did the most primitive light-sensitive cells come into being? Why is reality structured so that there can be a symbiosis between light and the eye, between photons and neurons, that results in sight? Light waves, incidentally, are the only kind of electromagnetic radiation with the energy level required for biological systems to detect them and the wavelength of light is just the right size for the high-resolution camera-type vertebrate eye.

Third, what lies at the basis of the amazing transformational interfaces between eye, brain and mind that convert electromagnetic waves into electrical signals and then into subjective visual images—activities that take place so effortlessly that we take them for granted?

In the operation of the five senses, seeing, hearing, smelling, tasting and touching, the fundamental event involved is the transformation

95 Cited in Matthew Cobb, *The Idea of the Brain: The Past and Future of Neuroscience,* op cit., 242. See also Horace Barlow, "Grandmother Cells, Symmetry, and Invariance: How the Term Arose and What the Facts Suggest" (Cambridge, MA: MIT Press, 2009).

of a mechanical stimulus into a nerve signal sent to the brain that is then converted into a conscious state.

But, despite decades of scientific study and progress made in understanding the network of proteins, ions, signals and cellular structures involved, the bridge between these two worlds, the external stimulus and the corresponding sense-perception, remains as much a mystery today as ever.

To be conscious is to be aware, to be in contact with the world in a manner that goes beyond the collision of material bodies or the interaction of physical fields. Awareness is found not simply in human beings but manifests itself in multiple modes across the spectrum of living organisms.

We certainly do not know what it is like to be a bat but we do know it has sensory organs and that it acts and reacts within its environment in ways indicating certain forms of awareness. Of course, we know ourselves best and I know my own experience best of all.

And what I know is that in some mysterious way I see, hear, feel, smell and taste. To be sure, this is only possible because I have eyes, ears, a nervous system and the like. But it is not my eyes that see or my ears that hear. It is I who sees and hears. We will presently consider the question of the "I" but first let us look at what it means to be conscious.

As an attribute, awareness is undeniable, unified, unique, irreducible and *mine* and cannot in any conceivable sense be described as physical or as connected in any way with the quantifiable world of science.

It is simply unintelligible to talk of our feeling of pain or our glimpse of the starry heavens as being five feet tall or weighing eight pounds.

Also to be considered is the unity of consciousness that we take for granted. As David Lund has said,

> "One of the greatest challenges for the reductionist is to provide a plausible account for the unity of consciousness. … [This is] the problem of understanding how several different simultaneous experiences can be held together in what seems to be a single consciousness. The challenge for the reductionist is to provide an account of what unifies a set of simultaneous experiences if there is no appeal to a single subject who has each member of the set." There is also the problem of how our identity being "maintained over substantial periods of time, should be understood."[96]
>
> "In first-person terms, the continuity of my experience provides me with a tacit knowledge of my continuous existence throughout a succession of experiences."
>
> "It seems undeniable that our knowledge of the unity of consciousness is grounded in immediate experience rather than in inference."[97]

Those who talk of consciousness in terms of feedback loops or mental modules or evolutionary adaptations seem to have left behind the primordial ground of their experience.

They need to step outside, hear the birds sing, feel the grass under their feet, smell the fragrance of a rose and then reflect on this concrete reality without hiding behind abstractions.

How is it possible to be "in touch" in this magical manner that defies description in the language of science?

To be sure there are multiple media at work behind the scenes, photons and neuronal networks, vibrations, electrical impulses and receptors. But none of these have the property of being conscious.

Cut open the brain and you cannot detect a feeling of pain. And neurons and all the structures in the brain are fundamentally just

96 David Lund, *The Conscious Self*, op cit. 49-50.

97 Ibid., 81.

manifestations of quantum fields and are therefore made of the same "material" as meteors and sand dunes.

Conscious events are mediated through certain structures but the events themselves belong to a different world from the structures. The firing of C-fibers is one thing, pain another.

One may transmit or "embody" the other but that does not mean they are one and the same thing. There can be no pain if there is no subject but there can be C-fiber firings with or without a subject; and the "feeling" of pain cannot be quantified like the C-fiber firing since there are no quantities involved in feelings.

Your decision to take a jog around the lake may be accompanied by activity in the hypothetical human mirror neuron system. But your cogitation on the matter is not the same thing as the associated firing of mirror neurons. There is no decision-making without a subject and, what is more, the process of making a decision cannot coherently be thought of as a physical activity, namely transmitting an electrical impulse. You might as well say that your decision-making is nothing more or less than shooting a missile.

On the one hand, conscious events are radically integrated with the physical infrastructure of our being but, on the other, they are not identical with this infrastructure. Some conscious events, for instance pain, are caused by our interaction with the environment but others, for instance our intentions or thoughts, cause such interaction. In both cases, there is a subject involved, a self, a "me," as we will see.

It is our consciousness that makes the world of our experience possible. Color, sound, smell, taste, and touch would not exist if not for consciousness. In the absence of conscious observers, the universe would be a colorless, soundless and odorless interaction of feature-less particles and energy fields.

THE CONSCIOUSNESS RESEARCH PROGRAM

The scientific investigation of consciousness has now become a major new research program.

In its "Why consciousness is the hardest problem in science" report, *Scientific American* notes that

> "Today there are dozens of competing theories of how the brain generates consciousness. They have different starting points, different goals and even different definitions of consciousness."

There are disagreements at fundamental levels:

> "Leading theories disagree on where consciousness comes from in the brain. Does conscious arise from frontal regions, especially the pre-frontal cortex, which is responsible for high-level processing and decision making [a claim made by Global Workspace Theory]? Or does it come from areas towards the back of the brain where information from different senses is integrated [the approach of Integrated Information Theory]? Pioneer researcher David Chalmers notes, "It's clear that things are not clear." It is clear that, "There's a chasm between our everyday experiences and what science can explain." Researcher Tim Bayne points out that "No one really has a theory that closes the explanatory gap."[98]

THE CONSCIOUSNESS "GAP"

Now how is it the case that consciousness exists? Certainly, none of the known laws of matter say anything about it. Consciousness cannot be measured, quantified or mathematically modeled and therefore is not scientifically treatable.

When we are dealing with consciousness, let alone thought or the self, we are not dealing with the standard problems treated by science.

98 "Why consciousness is the hardest problem in science," *Scientific American*, February 2026, https://www.scientificamerican.com/article/what-is-consciousness-science-faces-its-hardest-problem-yet/

All the other "gaps" filled by science—lightning, gravitation, the micro and macro structure of the universe, homologous structures in species—belong to the realm of the physical.

Since science is a methodology for studying anything that is quantifiable it is hardly surprising that it would solve "problems" involving quantities given enough time.

And also given "space"! Anything that occupies space or is perceptible in some fashion is by that very fact a candidate for scientific inquiry.

But thus far and no further.

If you are dealing with a reality that has no physical attributes then you cannot study it with a methodology that works only with the physical.

You might as well ask how Newton's laws of motion apply to the function of metaphor in poetry.

Neither a decade nor a million years is going to enable you to measure that which has neither dimension (size, shape, length, width) nor quanta of energy.

Naturalist philosopher Colin McGinn observes that consciousness does not occupy space thus deepening the mystery of its origin in space-time:

> "Nor do we think of conscious states as occupying an unperceived space, as we think of the unobservable entities of physics. We have no conception of what it would even be to perceive them as spatial entities. ... It is not that experiences have location, shape and dimensionality for eyes that are sharper than ours. *Since they are non-spatial they are in principle unperceivable.*"[99]

Nobel Laureate George Wald writes,

99 https://www.newdualism.org/papers/C.McGinn/ConsciousnessSpace.html

> "I had already for some time taken it as a foregone conclusion that the mind—consciousness—could not be located. It is essentially absurd to think of locating a phenomenon that yields no physical signals, the presence or absence of which - outside of humans and their like–cannot be identified.
>
> But further than that, mind is not only not locatable, it has no location. It is not a thing in space and time, not measurable; hence - as I said at the beginning of this paper—not assimilable as science."[100]

For this reason, Wald concludes,

> "Consciousness seems to me to be wholly impervious to science. It does not lie as an indigestible element within science, but just the opposite: Science is the highly digestible element within consciousness."[101]

Sir Brian Pippard, Cavendish Professor of Physics at Cambridge University, reiterates this last point:

> "The basic assumption of science is that there are certain facts of common observation on which all reasonable people can agree, and which repay communal investigation. These facts may include observations of the behaviour of individuals or societies, and even the expressed thoughts of individuals, but not what was going on in the conscious mind of the speaker.
>
> "For we have no means of entering into the consciousness of another, nor is there any manifest property of matter that gives the smallest clue to how conscious mind could come to be. ... Everything about the qualitative shift to consciousness remains enigmatic.[102]

100 1986 address to the First World Congress for the Synthesis of Science and Religion.

101 George Wald, "Life and Mind in the Universe," in Henry Margenau and Roy Abraham Varghese ed. *Cosmos, Bios, Theos* (La Salle: Open Court, 1992), 218.

102 https://www.lrb.co.uk/the-paper/v07/n10/brian-pippard/discontinuities

A New Reality

Consciousness represents a new reality in the universe.

In *How the Mind Works*, Pinker says we have no idea where sentience, i.e., *what consciousness feels like on the inside*, came from. Nor do we know how or why. He says that *neither the computational theory of mind nor any finding in neuroscience have an answer* to these basic questions about our subjective experience of consciousness. Saying that we have no scientific explanation of sentience, says Pinker, is not saying that sentience does not exist at all. "I am as certain that I am sentient as I am certain of *anything*."[103] He adds that sentience is not a combination of brain events or computational states.

McGinn says,

> "It looks as if with consciousness a new kind of reality has been injected into the universe, instead of just a recombination of the old realities.
>
> Even if minds showed no hint of design, the same old problem would exist: How can mere matter originate consciousness? How did evolution convert the water of biological tissue into the wine of consciousness? Consciousness seems like a radical novelty in the universe, not prefigured by the after-effects of the Big Bang, so how did it contrive to spring into being from what preceded it?"[104]

Jerry Fodor, widely acclaimed as the leading philosopher of mind of modern times, noted,

> "Periodically, Nobel laureates pronounce on the connections between consciousness and evolution, quantum mechanics, information theory, complexity theory, chaos theory and the activity of neural nets. Everybody gives lectures about consciousness to everybody else. But for all that, nothing has been ascertained with

---

103 Steven Pinker, *How the Mind Works* (New York: W.W. Norton, 1997), 131.

104 Colin McGinn, *The Mysterious Flame: Conscious Minds in a Material World* (New York: Basic Books, 1999), 13, 115.

> respect to the problem that everybody worries about most: what philosophers have come to call 'the hard problem'.
>
> The hard problem is this: it is widely supposed that the world is made entirely of mere matter, but how could mere matter be conscious? How, in particular, could a couple of pounds of grey tissue have experiences? … I think it's strictly true that we can't, as things stand now, so much as imagine the solution of the hard problem. … Philosophers used to think (some still do) that a bit of analytical tidying up would make the hard problem go away. But they were wrong to think that. There is hardly anything that we may not have to cut loose from before the hard problem is through with us."[105]

James Ross tells us why conscious events cannot even in principle be reduced to physical constituents:

> There cannot be a "reductive explanation of how we abstract the forms and structures of things to perceive things as 'such and such,' say, elephants. Abstraction is a natural condition of intelligent consciousness, even of intellectually limited humans. It does not decompose into neural operations.
>
> Nor is there a reductive explanation of how a distant tree is made present even by an animal's perception of it, even nonabstractly. Neither is there any physical or an analytic reduction of sensation or of consciousness.
>
> Those processes and states are not made up of or constituted out of other activities, the way a chair is made of pieces or a program of subroutines. For if they were reducible to components, either the components would have the ability (abstraction, perception, consciousness, sensation), or they would lack it.
>
> In the first case, the mystery would remain in a new place; in the second, the reduction would have to amount to the ability we recognize (e.g., consciousness) or we would not count as successful, and so the mystery would revive, about how that phenomenon comes from (apparently) wholly different ones. On any account,

105 http://www.lrb.co.uk/v29/n10/jerry-fodor/headaches-have-themselves

there will be a reductive gap somewhere."[106]

106 James F. Ross, *Thought and World* (Notre Dame: University of Notre Dame Press, 2008), 112.

Bots and Thoughts

"As a matter of fact, I am convinced that even much more is to be asserted: the concepts which arise in our thought and in our linguistic expressions are all—when viewed logically—the free creations of thought which cannot inductively be gained from sense experiences. This is not so easily noticed only because we have the habit of combining certain concepts and conceptual relations (propositions) so definitely with certain sense experiences that we do not become conscious of the gulf—logically unbridgeable—which separates the world of sensory experiences from the world of concepts and propositions.[107]

—*Albert Einstein, "Remarks on Bertrand Russell's Theory of Knowledge"*

"There doesn't seem to be anything like syntax in non-human animals and it is hard to imagine evolutionary forerunners of it. Equally obscure is the origin of semantics, of words and their meanings."[108]

—*Richard Dawkins, Unweaving the Rainbow*

"Charles Darwin argued in his 1871 book *The Descent of Man* that the difference between human and nonhuman minds is 'one of degree and not of kind.' … Mounting evidence indicates that, in contrast to Darwin's theory of a continuity of mind between humans and other species, a profound gap separates our intellect from the animal kind. …Our mind is very different from that of even our closest primate relatives and … we do not know much about how that difference came to be."[109]

— *"The Origin of the Mind," Scientific American.*

"Language seems unique to humans on two counts. First, we have a natural tendency to construct it and use it, which other animals do not. Second, we have a capacity for language that far surpasses that of any

107 Albert Einstein, "Remarks on Bertrand Russell's Theory of Knowledge", in *The Philosophy of Bertrand Russell*, P. A. Schilpp, ed., (New York: Tudor Publishing, 1944), 290.

108 Richard Dawkins, *Unweaving the Rainbow* (Boston, MA: Houghton Mifflin Company, 1998), 286 ff.

109 "The Origin of the Mind," *Scientific American*, September 2009, https://www.scientificamerican.com/article/origin-of-the-mind/

other animal, even if some basic semblances of symbols and grammar is possible in other apes."[110]

—*Max S. Bennett, A Brief History of Intelligence: Evolution, AI, and the Five Breakthroughs That Made Our Brains—A Neuroscience Framework for Understanding Future Machines*

"Nowhere among human cultures have we ever discovered a language that could be characterised as evolutionarily primitive, or in any significant respect more elementary than any other. Every language exists as a complete semiotic system in which all the basic functions of syntax and semantics are fully present and fully developed, and in which the capacity for symbolic thought plays an indispensable role.

"More to the point, perhaps, thus far no one has come close to reverse-engineering a truly pre-linguistic or inchoately linguistic system that might actually operate in the absence of any of those functions. Every attempt to reduce fully formed semiotic economies to more basic syntactic algorithms, in the hope of further reducing those to protosyntactic functions in the brain, founders upon the reefs of the indissoluble top-down hierarchy of language. No matter how basic the mechanism the linguist isolates, it exists solely within the sheltering embrace of a complete semiotic ecology."[111]

—*David Bentley Hart*

"No major conceptual innovation has been made in our overall understanding of how the brain works for over half a century. This period has seen immense, Nobel Prize winning discoveries ... All of this gives us a far richer understanding of what is happening where in the brain, compared with past generations, but we still think about the brain in the way our scientific grandparents did. … The immense success of our understanding of what the brain does is built on this common approach that was established in the 1940s and early 1950s."[112]

—*Matthew Cobb, The Idea of the Brain: The Past and Future of Neuroscience*

"fMRI cannot tell us what single cells, or networks of cells, are up to. Even at the level of neural tracts, it cannot tell us meaningfully what

---

110 Max S. Bennett, *A Brief History of Intelligence: Evolution, AI, and the Five Breakthroughs That Made Our Brains—A Neuroscience Framework for Understanding Future Machines* (New York: Mariner Books, 2023), 301.

111 https://www.abc.net.au/religion/david-bentley-hart-narcissus-reflections-on-ai/102812590

112 Matthew Cobb, *The Idea of the Brain: The Past and Future of Neuroscience*, op cit., 201.

is happening, merely where, at an extremely coarse level, something is happening relatively more or less than elsewhere. Perhaps."[113]

—*Matthew Cobb, The Idea of the Brain: The Past and Future of Neuroscience*

"For almost three decades, functional magnetic resonance imaging (fMRI) has been one of the main tools in brain research. Yet a new study published in the renowned journal *Nature Neuroscience* fundamentally challenges the way fMRI data have so far been interpreted with regard to neuronal activity. According to the findings, there is no generally valid coupling between the oxygen content measured by MRI and neuronal activity. … First author Dr. Samira Epp emphasizes: "This contradicts the long-standing assumption that increased brain activity is always accompanied by an increased blood flow to meet higher oxygen demand. *Since tens of thousands of fMRI studies worldwide are based on this assumption, our results could lead to opposite interpretations in many of them* [emphasis added]."[114]

— *"40 percent of MRI signals do not correspond to actual brain activity," Nature Neuroscience Research Report*

"I've had thousands of patients with damaged or disfigured brains yet pretty good minds. Thus, I learned that there are parts of the brain that don't seem to matter in everyday life. … When I studied the work of fellow neurosurgeons and neuroscientists, I learned that the ability to the mind to reason never shows up in brain seizures and can never be evoked by stimulating the brain with an electrical probe. … Reason itself doesn't seem to come from the brain—at least not in the same way that movement, sensation, and memory come from the brain."[115]

—*Michael Egnor (and Denyse O'Leary), The Immortal Mind: A Neurosurgeon's Case for the Existence of the Soul*

"Assumptions about highly localised bits of our brain representing particular words or concepts are wrong. To the extent that fMRI can truly provide an answer to this kind of question, those functions seem to be distributed across different parts of the brain."[116]

—*Matthew Cobb, The Idea of the Brain: The Past and Future of Neuroscience*

---

113 Ibid., 319.

114 https://www.tum.de/en/news-and-events/all-news/press-releases/details/40-percent-of-mri-signals-do-not-correspond-to-actual-brain-activity. Story on a research report in *Nature Neuroscience*, December 2025. https://www.nature.com/articles/s41593-025-02132-9

115 Denyse O'Leary and Michael Egnor, *The Immortal Mind: A Neurosurgeon's Case for the Existence of the Soul* (New York: Worthy Books, 2025), 182.

116 Matthew Cobb, *The Idea of the Brain: The Past and Future of Neuroscience*, op cit., 322.

"It is hopeless to try to solve conceptual problems concerning the nature of consciousness by empirical methods. PET and fMRI can scan brains but not concepts and their articulation. Neuroscience can investigate synaptic connections but not conceptual ones."[117]

—*M.R. Bennett and P.M.S. Hacker*

"The brain is vital to us as bodily beings if our understanding is to find expression in speech and in coordination with perception, imagination, memory, emotion and action. But the role of the brain is rather to facilitate our expression of understanding and thinking in the medium of words than to embody it. Our thinking is not *embodied* in language, but *expressed* using it; nor is it embodied in neural or imaginative sequences. The activities of understanding, thinking and questioning, with their nonrepresentational character, combined with our freedom in the exercise of the capacity involved exhibited in the lack of definable limits to the flexibility in our use of words, show that these activities cannot be the work of any bodily organ. This does not make them the work of some other organ, but the activities of the person as such.

It is the way linguistic understanding, thinking and questioning transcend the body and transcend limitations set by the body which is of peculiar importance for the status of human beings. For, since what acts exists, and these human activities transcend the body, human existence must therefore also transcend the body."[118]

—*David Braine, Language and Human Understanding*

"Intellectual activity— the forming of ideas or concepts, the making of judgments, and logical reasoning—is an essentially immaterial process, a process that is intrinsically independent of matter, however much it may be *extrinsically* dependent on matter for its normal operations in the human being."[119]

—*David Oderberg, "Hylemorphic Dualism"*

"Mind, meaning by that thoughts, memory, feelings, reasoning, and so

117 *Philosophical Foundations of Neuroscience* (Oxford: Blackwell Publishing, 2003), 405.

118 David Braine, *Language and Human Understanding* (Washington D.C.: CUA Press, 2014), 67.

119 David Oderberg, "Hylemorphic Dualism" in Ellen Frankel Paul, Fred Dycus Miller, Jeffrey Paul (eds), *Personal identity*, 70-99.

on, is difficult to bring into a class of physical things."[120]

—*Charles Sherrington, the "father of neurophysiology"*

"The mind must be viewed as a basic element in itself … That is to say it has a continuing existence."[121]

—*Pioneering neurosurgeon Wilder Penfield*

We have seen that none of the laws of matter describe or explain how it is possible to be conscious. But we are not just conscious.

We also have *thoughts* and *intentions*. These are what drive our neurons and not the other way around.

And when we use language, we are encoding and decoding signals and processing *meaning*. But matter and its laws know nothing of meaning or reasons or purposes.

Conceptual thought thus cannot be identified with the world of matter. Thoughts are not neural bots.

There are two kinds of thought—those related to the things we touch and feel and see and those that are abstract.

We talked earlier about percepts—what we perceive with the senses—and concepts—what we "abstract" from our sense-perceptions.

Sense-perception is inter-twined with physical processes. Something in the physical world, for instance photons, interacts with our anatomy, our neurons, and the result is a sense-perception.

Conceptual thought, on the other hand, cannot be correlated with the physical. Our thoughts about human rights are not generated by

120 Charles Sherrington quoted in Wilder Penfield, *The Mystery of the Mind* (Princeton: Princeton University Press, 1975), xxv.

121 Wilder Penfield, *The Mystery of the Mind* (Princeton: Princeton University Press, 1975) xxi.

particles or fields. The traffic is entirely one-way. Concepts produce neural firings instead of the other way round.

As Einstein highlighted, there is a difference of kind between the operations of our senses–sensory consciousness–and our intellectual operations. A toothache is a sensation we feel. The dentist's account of the toothache involves concepts such as "cause"—perhaps a cavity—and "prevention" (no candy!). And concepts are not sensations.

Just as clearly, our thoughts have a life of their own. They cannot coherently be thought of as physical processes or bots. For instance, our reflections on the promotion of liberty in society are not theatrical productions directed by action potentials and sodium ions. They are driven rather by reasoning and analysis.

Conceptual thought in our experience requires a brain. But aren't particular kinds of thought restricted to certain regions of the brain? Don't we know that a blow to the head or a hallucinogenic drug or a neurological disorder drastically changes our thinking capabilities? Don't scans show how the brain processes various kinds of thought? And doesn't this mean that thought—conceptual or otherwise—is ultimately just a physical process?

We should and will consider the relation between conceptual thought and what we know of the brain. But we should start off with an understanding of what is necessary for thought and what is sufficient.

A functioning brain is *necessary* for thought just as an operational cell phone is necessary to make a call. But the physical processes of the brain are not *sufficient* to describe let alone explain the meaning-processing carried out by its intellectual agent-user. Likewise, the intellectual content of a call from a user is transmitted but not created by the phone: the phone is necessary but not sufficient for the call.

Like our undeniable awareness of being aware, the non-physical nature of conceptual thought is self-evident in immediate experience. It is not an inference from data but part of the raw data itself.

To see why, we can use two descriptions of fundamental human actions as our road-map: "I understand" and "I intend."

No-brainers

What do we mean by "I," "understand" and "intend?" There is no physical organ, no region of the brain where you can find the "I," "understanding" or "intending."

Once you recognize the reality of the "I"; its capability of "understanding," of decoding and encoding, of "seeing meaning"; and its ability to "intend," you recognize as well the integrated unity of physical and non-physical that is the human person.

Nobody can deny (without instantly contradicting themselves) that the phrases "I understand" and "I intend" are true statements about actual states of affairs. These phrases involve three mysterious realities: the I, meaning and intention.

Equally, nobody can deny that these three states of affairs are not a description of electrical or chemical realities. So how do we explain their existence? What is their locus of being?

Certainly, there is neuronal activity accompanying all our thinking and intending. But what neuroscientists call the "neural code" concerns only the relation between physical stimuli and action potentials; it can say nothing about the conceptual content of our thoughts. We do know, however, that none of this neuronal activity is a "translation" or "representation" of what we are thinking about or intending. The idea that there could be a physical counterpart of our concept of liberty is incoherent.

The question before us is this. How can a physical being perform non-physical operations that, by their nature, are qualitatively distinct from and sometimes entirely independent of the physical?

All the "data" generated by the senses concern that which is physical. But this is not the case in language and understanding: meaning is fundamental.

If we were to consider the virtue of thrift, our whole train of thought is not entirely a matter of neurons and photons or biochemistry and electricity.

Although physical processes play a role, the weighing of the pros and cons is not in any coherent sense physical—and of course there is an "I" who does the weighing.

From start to finish, the whole train of thought is an exercise of conceptual processing driven not by sights and sounds but meanings, insights and inferences.

We are forced to recognize a subject, a person, engaged in an activity that belongs to a different world from the physical.

This takes us to the central issue we face: what and where is the "I" and how does it understand and intend.

These questions clearly cannot be addressed by studying the brain, given that the molecules in each neuron are replaced thousands of times over one's lifetime and there can therefore be no physical basis for an enduring, identical self. Neuroscientists who once thought they could find an "I" structure in the brain now admit that there is no such structure.

Conscious activity may be correlated with neural processes but correlation is one thing and cause another.

If your cell phone is powered up, you can hear the person on the other end: but does the correlation between the cell phone being powered up and your ability to hear your caller prove that being powered up "causes" the conversation?

Even the analogy of cell phones fails to convey what is happening. Here one physical signal (our speech) is converted into another (electromagnetic radiation). We are talking about the conversion of one form of physical energy into another not about a unified psychophysical act performed by a unitary subject.

What exactly is happening in the brain?

Electrical discharges and chemical reactions LITERALLY and that is all.

There is an insuperable barrier between the world of electro-chemical interactions, anatomical structures and genomic blueprints on the one hand and the world of meanings and intentions on the other. Genes and neurons do not "understand" or "intend."

Even less intelligible is it to talk about an "I" as a genetic or neuronic creation or reality.

So what is this I? As we will see shortly, it is that which unifies. It is conscious, it remains the same, it gives you your first person perspective.

Our focus here is on "understanding" and we turn now to its most obvious vehicles, language and concepts.

Language and "Understanding"

> "Linguistic understanding and thinking within human life always involve brain processes but can never consist in them. Many lines of argument, including some from Wittgenstein, converge on the conclusion that a proposition, that is, a sentence of the kind that

> can be true or false, cannot represent or be [identical in structure, i.e,,"isomorphic"] with what it purports to report. Equally, it cannot be [identical/isomorphic] with any state or process in the brain. Equally also, the meanings of such sentences cannot be represented by any state or process in the brain. ... It is the way in which human acts of judging and understanding, lacking any [identity/"isomorphism"] with any bodily process, exemplify the command of the intellect, not the determinism of the physical, in our linguistic expressions of judgment and understanding which provides our clearest demonstrations of how human beings transcend the body."[122]
>
> —*David Braine, Language and Human Understanding*

As we have seen, language presupposes our capability for conceptual thought as well as a community of people in which a particular language makes sense.

In his works, David Braine has shown that *linguistic understanding* is a complete act of its own. It has no bodily organ and excludes any bodily activity from being internal to it. Understanding and thinking in the medium of words "are 'operations' of the human being which have no inner neural realization: they have a bodily expression in speech, and are typically directed towards bodily objects (bodily things as real or intentional objects), but are not operations of any bodily organ."[123]

Braine's major point is that thought expressed in language and the understanding of language "cannot have any physical process internal to them as physical processes are internal to perception, imagining, emotion, and intentional action." He gives four reasons for this position.[124]

---

122 David Braine, *Language and Human Understanding*, op cit., 20-1.

123 David Braine, *The Human Person—Animal and Spirit*, (Notre Dame: University of Notre Dame Press, 1994), 537.

124 Ibid., 449, 450, 459, 451, 461, 451.

It is the person who speaks and understands	In thinking expressed in words whether in writing or speech, "it is the person or human who understands, speaks and hears, and thinks, and these are not operations of some inner part of him or her but of the person him or herself."
The power of conceptual thinking	The use of general concepts cannot be emulated by any material process or state because what is required is "a capacity or principle of operation making it possible for the human being to grasp the essence of the likeness" between different instances of the same concept, e.g., knowing what are the features common to different humans. Physical structures in the brain or images of various humans will not do the job since we have to "stand back" from all humans and make a judgment on what is alike about them using our understanding.
Use of language involves indefinite number of ways of using words	Linguistic expression and understanding require us "to use words in an indefinite number of logically distinguishable types of use." This cannot be correlated with any physical organ or process "because any supposed correlate would lack the flexibility, or extensibility in type of relation to different types of case, which is required." "The fact that understanding explains something, without there being a deterministic mechanical process involved, is shown by the impossibility of calculating rather than 'seeing' meaning."
Language requires a subject capable of self-reflection	The capacity for language or linguistic understanding or for thought in the medium of words requires "a judging subject and within it structures of self-reflection and of reflection on procedures of coming to judgements." This structure has to be unitary while incorporating these sub-systems. No mechanically operating system can emulate these structures and also the ability to critically reflect cannot be tied to any physical process internal to it.

Our use of language obviously has physical components: sounds, sights, speech organs, scripts, gestures, neural connections to our speech and hearing, memory of vocabulary, use of various "parts" of the brain for various kinds of linguistic processing (e.g., tense forms, plurals).

At the lower levels of language use, we can plausibly suggest that specific areas of the brain are specialized for certain functions. But at the higher levels, the use of language is constrained less by the hardware than it is by constraints like semantics.

Braine documents the ways in which the brain serves the intellect:

> "The brain and any other bodily apparatus subserving our use of language have evolved biologically in such a way as to become malleable in their modes of functioning as to be open to the workings of intellect.
>
> That is, these modes of functioning have become such as to be shaped by the semantic and pragmatic structures of our speaking and hearing, rather than themselves determining these semantic and pragmatic structures. … Within this framework it is semantic syntax which shapes particular "mechanisms" in the use of language—for instance, mechanisms for vocabulary structure and recovery. …
>
> When a person makes a judgment, this process or action is not mediated by "representations" whether in the brain or mind or in language, and the function of linguistic expression is to *express* such judgment, not to *represent* it … and not to give it [a] … neurological embodiment. This is part of what puts the intellect in command."[125]

Perception and imagination, stimulus and response, vocabulary and morphology—all these are tied to the physical milieu that is the brain. Not so semantics or concepts, meaning or understanding.

We have noted that it makes no sense to speak of conceptually-driven understanding or of concepts and meaning as manifestations or by-products of physical processes.

While physical media can serve as vehicles *through* which we understand, understanding itself is not a physical process like the release of a chemical neurotransmitter. Even more clearly outside the physicalist web is the subject who understands, integrates and responds, the understander.

125 David Braine, *Language and Human Understanding*, op cit., 19.

Braine highlights the unitary character of language:

> "The unitariness of the semantic structure of language … is such as to exclude the idea of human language as developing, either characteristic by characteristic, or structural element by structural element, as if by a process of gradual addition of characteristics or structural elements to some pre-existing whole, language might have developed bit by bit until it has reached the rounded whole shared by all human beings, so far as they are adult and unimpaired in faculties. Rather, human beings' simplest judgments, even "James is eating", would lack the meaning they have for a person of unimpaired faculties if the person was not able to understand the difference between being actual and merely possible, and understand the raising of questions as to truth or falsehood, certainty and uncertainty, all implying the capacity to reflect and deliberate. …
>
> In this way the human capacity for speech involves the whole of the intellectual structure met with in language. New forms of experience may be met with and new vocabulary learnt and understood but the framework of understanding into which any judgment about experience or within which any vocabulary is utilized is unitary, and likewise the linguistic framework which reflects this understanding. In this way, the human language capacity … unlike other developments seen in evolution towards human kind has an all at once or nothing character, even though the development of its external realization is dependent on the development of linguistic exchange within a community." [126]

Ironically, physicalism is a form of Cartesian dualism. Braine writes,

> "Any such conception of the mental as having its only … realization in the brain involves the Cartesian severance of the mental, thought of as realized only in or through brain states and processes, from the behavioral and perceptual with their aspects outside the brain." He adds that this position was rejected by philosophers of

126 David Braine, "Life and Human Life" in Roy Abraham Varghese, ed., *The Missing Link* (Lanham, MD: University Press of America, 2013), 141-2.

> language like Wittgenstein and J.L. Austin. The understanding involved in language possession and language use "should be integral to the ultimate explanation of the things we do in expressing our judgment—understanding and judgment both being things which involve mind."[127]

Language is a manifestation of conceptual thought but (contrary to the position taken by some philosophers) thought precedes language. Once we consider conceptual thought on its own terms we are compelled to recognize its intrinsically immaterial nature.

As we saw, James Ross highlights the fact that intellection precedes linguistic activity:

> Intelligence, understanding, explanatorily *precedes* language. ... Expressive capacity belongs to the medium, but expressive ability belongs to the thinkers. Abstractive ability is native, not learned, but abstractive practices are learned and are socially refined."[128]

Meaning-processing is central to the use of language. We process meaning with concepts.

Concepts and the Intellect That Houses Them Are Not Physical

Whatever we know about the world we know through concepts. We notice differences and similarities between things and generalize and universalize from this. Thomas Sullivan points out that all human thought revolves around our ability to effortlessly think of universal characteristics that can have local instances, for instance the ideas of hot and blue. This is clearly an immaterial activity because these ideas are not linked to something physical (for instance, we do not have to think of a blue object when we think of blueness).

127 David Braine, *Language and Human Understanding*, op cit., 367.

128 James F. Ross, *Thought and the World*, op cit., 162.

David Oderberg has shown that concepts cannot have a physical locus because:

> humans have concepts and there is no physical way to "store" concepts and so the brain cannot be the locus of concepts
>
> if the intellect is essentially immaterial, all its operations have an immaterial locus: this includes not just understanding but perceiving and remembering
>
> since the human person is essentially embodied these immaterial operations usually operate with the material
>
> nevertheless the immaterial operations can continue solely with the immaterial locus (albeit in an impoverished fashion) if there is a separation of the material and the immaterial.

As Oderberg elaborates, the intellect has to be immaterial if its operations are immaterial:

> "The reason for the proposition that the intellect is immaterial is that there is an essential ontological mismatch between the proper objects of intellectual activity just mentioned and any kind of potential physical embodiment of them: we might call this the *embodiment problem*, but looked at in a slightly narrower way, in cognitive-scientific terms, it might be called the location or storage problem.
>
> Concepts, propositions, and arguments are abstract; potential material loci for these items are concrete. The former are unextended; the latter are extended. The former are universals; the latter are particular. Nothing that is abstract, unextended, and universal—and it is perhaps hard to see how anything abstract could be other than unextended and universal—could be embodied, located, or stored in anything concrete, extended, and particular. Therefore, the proper objects of intellectual activity can have no material embodiment or locus. …
>
> The intellect is capable of grasping a potential infinity of concepts,

> but no corporeal organ can harbor a potential infinity of anything. In particular, the intellect is distinguished by this feature: that it can grasp a potentially infinite number of *categories* of concepts, and within each category a potentially infinite number of exemplars. In other words, there is no limit to the number of kinds of things the intellect can recognize, and no limit to the number of examples of each kind that it can grasp. By contrast, the eye or ear, for instance, can only receive colors and sounds, respectively; and within each kind of sense datum, they can only receive a limited number of examples—hence, we cannot naturally see certain colors or hear certain sounds."[129]

Physicalists may (at the risk of self-contradiction) respond that we do not possess concepts. But, as Oderberg says, this would result in "an inability to explain fundamental semantic and logical phenomena: not merely the fact that the concept of a black dog is a function of the concept of black and the concept of dog, but that the *concept-possessor* understands this ... [This] means that if he has those concepts, he can *see* how one is derived from the others." The same holds true for judgments and inferences.[130]

The Biography of Language

When it comes to animals, there is no use of concepts, no "meaning" embodied and communicated through a variety of arbitrary symbols. Of course, animals have emotions, responses, instincts and other forms of cognition focused on physically observable objects. And animal communication and instinct are a marvel to behold. But conceptual processing and the encoding and decoding of meaning are entirely absent.

129 David Oderberg, "Hylemorphic Dualism," op cit., 70-99.

130 Ibid., 70-99.

"The Origin of the Mind," published in *Scientific American*, points to four areas where human thought is fundamentally different from cognition in other animals:

> "Generative computation" which is the ability "to create a virtually limitless variety of 'expressions.'" These include "arrangements of words, sequences of notes, combinations of actions, or strings of mathematical symbols."
>
> The mind's capacity for promiscuously combining ideas.
>
> The ability to use mental symbols whereby humans spontaneously convert sensory experiences into symbols.
>
> "Only humans engage in abstract thought." Animal mental life, however, is "largely anchored in sensory and perceptual experiences."[131]

Max Bennett observes that

> "There is no language organ in the human brain, just as there is no flight organ in the bird brain. Asking where language lives in the brain may be as silly as asking where playing baseball or playing guitar lives in the brain. Such complex skills are not localized to a specific area; they emerge from a complex interplay of many areas. What makes these skills possible is not a single region that executes them but a curriculum that forces a complex network of regions to work together to *learn* them. So this is why your brain and a chimp brain are practically identical and yet only humans have language. … Language, at least as far as we know, has emerged only once."[132]

How did language arise? This question was comprehensively addressed by such leading evolutionary scientists as Richard Lewontin and Ian Tattersall and the founding father of modern linguistics, Noam Chomsky. In their paper "The mystery of language evolution," they

131 "The Origin of the Mind," op cit.

132 Max S. Bennett, *A Brief History of Intelligence: Evolution, AI, and the Five Breakthroughs That Made Our Brains—A Neuroscience Framework for Understanding Future Machines,* op cit., 321-2.

conclude that we know virtually nothing about the origin of language, a distinctive feature of the human species:

> "Understanding the evolution of language requires evidence regarding origins and processes that led to change. In the last 40 years, there has been an explosion of research on this problem as well as a sense that considerable progress has been made. We argue instead that the richness of ideas is accompanied by a poverty of evidence, with essentially no explanation of how and why our linguistic computations and representations evolved.
>
> We show that, to date, (1) studies of nonhuman animals provide virtually no relevant parallels to human linguistic communication, and none to the underlying biological capacity; (2) the fossil and archaeological evidence does not inform our understanding of the computations and representations of our earliest ancestors, leaving details of origins and selective pressure unresolved; (3) our understanding of the genetics of language is so impoverished that there is little hope of connecting genes to linguistic processes any time soon; (4) all modeling attempts have made unfounded assumptions, and have provided no empirical tests, thus leaving any insights into language's origins unverifiable.
>
> Based on the current state of evidence, we submit that the most fundamental questions about the origins and evolution of our linguistic capacity remain as mysterious as ever, with considerable uncertainty about the discovery of either relevant or conclusive evidence that can adjudicate among the many open hypotheses."[133]

Brain Waves

Ever since modern neuroscience began in earnest with the development of fMRI, it was assumed that sooner or later we would find the neural bases of wisdom, love, reasoning, and other human activities.

133 *Front. Psychol.*, 07 May 2014, https://www.frontiersin.org/articles/10.3389/fpsyg.2014.00401/full

As we have seen in the introductory citations, these assumptions have turned out to be demonstrably wrong–or, as we could also put it, not even wrong!

Cobb focuses on "the fundamental weakness of fMRI—it is too coarse to allow a real understanding of the computational activity of the brain."[134]

Attempts to localize the language function in the brain did not end well.

> "Even the simplest animal brain is not homogenous but has a highly developed internal structure—but in most cases a single function cannot be precisely localised to a given area; for the function to exist, that region needs to be integrated into a functional whole."[135]
>
> "Structures in the brain are not modules that are isolated from one another ... This presumably underlies some examples of plasticity and emphasises the difficulty of precisely identifying functions with a given location ... These data give us a glimpse into the complexity of the brain, and how it uses both localised and distributed functions, even though the actual circuits used remain a mystery.[136]

In one instance of fanciful extrapolation, the neuroscientist Marco Iacoboni drew conclusions about the political leanings of his subjects on the basis of brain imaging data. But this attempt, described in a *New York Times* article titled "This is Your Brain on Politics", met with a well-deserved rebuke from fifteen of the world's leading neuroscientists.

> "As cognitive neuroscientists who use the same brain imaging technology, we know that it is not possible to definitively determine whether a person is anxious or feeling connected simply by looking at activity in a particular brain region. This is so because brain regions are typically engaged by many mental states, and thus a one-to-one mapping between a brain region and a mental state

---

134 Matthew Cobb, *The Idea of the Brain: The Past and Future of Neuroscience*, op cit., 320.

135 Ibid., 331.

136 Ibid., 334-5.

> is not possible.[137]

According to Patricia Churchland, who is herself a physicalist,

> "Mental modules are complete nonsense. There are no modules that are encapsulated and just send information into a central processor. There are areas of specialization, yes, and networks maybe, but these are not always dedicated to a particular task."[138]

With regard to the relevance of fMRI for concepts, Oderberg writes,

> "If researchers into functional imaging have shown anything, then, it is merely that category-specific object recognition is correlated with activity in certain distinct, if highly diffuse and non-discrete, regions in the brain. But this sort of research, as interesting and as potentially useful for braindamaged patients as it might be, goes no way to even beginning to provide a theoretical or empirical foundation for the idea that concepts, judgments, and inferences themselves have a physical location."[139]

Neural and Conceptual Processing

Neuroscience has been helpful in shedding new light on the nature of conceptual processing. As neurosurgeon Michael Egnor writes,

> "There was a key exception to what [pioneering neurosurgeon Wilder] Penfield could stimulate in the brain. He was never able to stimulate abstract thought—that is, the sense of self, the capacity to reason, and the exercise of free will. Natural seizures didn't produce that sort of abstract thought either. ... Penfield was not saying that seizures involving ideas are uncommon; his point was that they *never* occurred. Neither epilepsy nor neurosurgeons, it seems, could evoke abstract intellectual thought by stimulating

137 "Politics and the Brain," *New York Times*, November 14, 2007. http://query.nytimes.com/gst/fullpage.html?res=9907E1D91E3CF937A25752C1A9619C8B63

138 Patricia Churchland, "How Do Neurons Know?," *Daedalus*, Winter 2004, 44.

139 David Oderberg, "Hylemorphic Dualism," op cit.

> the brain."[140]

We have also come to see that there is a radical distinction between neural and conceptual processing.

Linguist Mark Baker begins with Chomsky's classic categorization of the language faculty into three components:

> "the lexicon (a list of words), the grammar (a set of rules for combining words) and … the 'Creative Aspect of Language Use' or CALU." CALU is "the ability to choose which words to use and assemble them in ways that are consistent with the grammar to make actual sentences." CALU when applied to the production and interpretation of language is unbounded, stimulus-free and appropriate.

Baker holds that there is no evidence

> "that the CALU capacity to use vocabulary and grammar to create and understand an unlimited number of new and appropriate sentences is biological in nature.
>
> More specifically, there is no evidence from aphasia that it is neurologically embodied, no evidence from developmental disorders that it is genetically encoded, and no evidence that it evolved from something that we have in common with closely related primates.
>
> Seen with an openness to the Soul Hypothesis, it seems appropriate, then, to think that grammar and vocabulary depend at least in part on the body, but the CALU depends primarily upon another ingredient of human nature, the soul." [141]

---

140 Michael Egnor (and Denyse O'Leary), *The Immortal Mind: A Neurosurgeon's Case for the Existence of the Soul*, op cit., 31.

141 Mark C. Baker, "Brains and Souls; Grammar and Speaking" in Mark C. Baker and Stewart Goetz (eds.), *The Soul Hypothesis* (New York: Continuum, 2011), 77-91.

Which Came First—the Bot or the Thought?

In considering conceptual thought, we realize that it is not bots that drive our thoughts. Our neuronal processes are driven by our conscious intentions and intellectual operations. This insight comes to us not just from immediate experience but also from neuroscience.

The Nobel Prize-winning neuroscientist Roger Sperry discovered from his experiments that the conscious mind controls brain events.

As Sperry put it:

> "The more I learn about the workings of the brain and how it processes information, the stronger becomes my allegiance to the type of truth that receives consistent empirical validation in the outside real world. … As a brain scientist, I have come to believe in the reality and power of conscious mental/cognitive entities of the mind or spirit and the indispensability of their causal control for both brain function and its evolution. …
>
> The shift from a noncausal to a causal view of consciousness, asserting that subjective awareness counts and makes a real difference in the physical world, has enormous and far-reaching implications. …
>
> The shift of mental qualities from a noncausal to a causal status demanded basic revisions in our prior materialist/behaviorist convictions. Brain function could no longer be thought to be fully explainable in terms of its chemistry or molecular biology. The higher organizational network properties must also be included as irreducible control factors. Instead of excluding mind and spirit, this view retains all the rich subjective qualities as integral and ineliminable functional agents, …
>
> The physical and chemical forces in the brain, though still present and operating as before, are enveloped or embedded within, and thereby controlled and programmed ('pushed and hauled around') by the higher laws and dynamics of conscious and subconscious mental processes. …

Brain-cell excitation, in this view, no longer waits solely on biophysical forces but also obeys a higher command, involving subjective feelings, wants, choices, intentions, moral values, and all other things of the mind. The subjective events of mind and consciousness have their own dynamics and laws of causal progression. These transcend and control the events of brain physiology in an enveloping supervenient sense."[142]

142 Roger W. Sperry, "A Search for Beliefs to Live by Consistent with Science," op cit., 314, 320, 323.

Me and My Self

"No one can assent to the thought that he does not exist. For in thinking something, he perceives that he exists."[143]

—*Thomas Aquinas, De Veritate*

"The conscious self is the center of consciousness and agency, it has a primitive matter-of-fact unity, and it maintains a "strict" identity through time. It is known, in the first instance, only from the first-person viewpoint, as it is directly known in one's experience of being a conscious subject and conscious agent. …

The conscious self is a subject of conscious states, capable of attaining the level of self-awareness manifested in its awareness that *it itself* is the subject of certain thoughts and the agent of certain deliberate actions. I is the referent of *I* when it uses that word in a self-referring way."[144]

—*David Lund, The Conscious Self*

"Just as we cannot identify and individuate mental states except by reference to the self whose mental states they are, so too we cannot identify and individuate person-stages except by reference to the person whose stages they are. Hence the attempt to reduce persons to collections of person-stages, like the attempt to reduce the self to a bundle of mental states, simply gets things the wrong way around."[145]

—*Edward Feser, Immortal Souls—A Treatise on Human Nature*

"To quote Margolis: 'Only the utter elimination of experience could possibly vindicate the elimination of selves.' … At its most primitive, self-experience is simply a question of being pre-reflectively aware of one's own consciousness, and the experiential self in question is precisely defined as the very subjectivity of experience."[146]

—*Dan Zahavi, Self and Other*

143 Thomas Aquinas, *De Veritate* (Q10, a12, ad7).

144 David Lund, *The Conscious Self*, op cit., 9.

145 Edward Feser, *Immortal Souls—A Treatise on Human Nature* (Neunkirchen-Seelscheid, Germany: Editions Scholasticae, 2024), 31.

146 Dan Zahavi, *Self and Other* (Oxford, UK: Oxford University Press, 2014), 24.

> "Consciousness does not *constitute* personhood; rather, it *presupposes and reveals* it."[147]
>
> —*David Oderberg*

> "The uniquely vivid quality of *my* experience remains unexplained. This reply is devastating to any theory of consciousness that fits within science as we now know it, because that science is built from a third-person perspective."[148]
>
> —*Andrew Ross "First-Person Consciousness"*

> "The 'I' is not a combination of body parts or brain states or bits of information, but a unity of selfness over time, a single locus that is nowhere in particular."[149]
>
> —*Steven Pinker*

WE ASK: WHAT IS it that perceives and conceives, feels and thinks, judges and chooses? It is me, I, my self.

The reality of the self is, well, self-evident. I cannot deny that I exist for the simple reason that the denial of the "I" requires the existence of an "I" who does the denying.

The self is not some mysterious esoteric entity that can only be discovered through metaphysics or meditation. In essence,

> It is the unifier of our consciousness, our experiences, our physical being
>
> It maintains our continued self-identity over the course of our lives (individual brain cells are just as incapable as the chips in a computer to serve as a self).
>
> It "constitutes" the body but not vice versa

147 David Oderberg, "Hylemorphic Dualism," op cit.

148 J. Andrew Ross, "First-Person Consciousness," *Journal of Consciousness Studies*, **9**, No. 7, 2002, 260.

149 *How the Mind Works* (New York: W.W. Norton, 1997), 564.

> It is the basis on which we act as self-conscious free agents. Moreover, the sense of responsibility possessed by all human persons can only be explained in terms of a self and not in Darwinian or Pavlovian terms.

I see, not my eyes. I think, not my brain. And the "I" that does the seeing and thinking remains the same throughout our lifetimes.

Nothing is more obvious about everyday experience than the fact that it is not experience unless there is an experiencer. Likewise there can no subjective experience if there is no subject.

All experiences are experiences of a subject. There are no subjectless experiences. There can be no thinking without a thinker, no seeing without the see-er. As the hallowed logician Gottlob Frege observed, "An experience is impossible without an experient."

Thus, experiences by their nature call for the existence of the self:

> "Not only does the notion of an individual subjectless experience seem unintelligible, but an adequate explanation of the synchronic unity of consciousness must include an appeal to the consciousness of a single subject. Perhaps even more importantly, the reality of a subject of consciousness could hardly be more securely established if, as I have contended, one has a prereflective self-awareness that must be understood to be the self-awareness of a subject of conscious states."[150]

Although we sometimes associate specific brain events with various mental acts, these correlations do not include the most fundamental mental reality, the "I" who is conscious and does the thinking.

The "I" is not present in any region of the brain.

---

150 David Lund, *The Conscious Self*, op. cit., 386.

Now some people assume or say that it is the brain or a part of the brain that is solely responsible for their mental activities. But this is clearly not the case if we go by our immediate experience.

When you think, see or act, it is YOU who are doing it.

You are thinking, not your brain (although the brain supports your thinking as does your circulatory system). You are seeing not your eye.

But this "I" cannot be described or experienced except as the radically mysterious reality that unifies my experiences, drives my actions and thinks my thoughts. You cannot reduce it to anything simpler or more basic.

It is the "I" that makes me inevitably think and speak with the first person perspective: *my* body, *my* thoughts, *my* intention.

There is nothing like a first person perspective in the physical world or the world of science.

What does it mean to be me, to experience something as myself? The question cannot even be described in physical terms and is not graspable by science although it is a fact of our everyday experience.

We cannot analyze the self because it is not a mental state that can be observed or described. We become aware of ourselves, said one philosopher, just in being ourselves and not in special states of self-consciousness.

Although we are not conscious of the self separate from its acts, we are conscious of it as the ground that suffuses and unifies our acts, the "center" that thinks, wills and feels.

How do I know the self exists? Well, first I have to become aware that I am aware, conscious that I am conscious and cognizant of my cognition.

What is most obvious in my everyday experience is the fact that I do experience things—and that this "I" which does the experiencing exists and that its experiences are "my" experiences.

I am directly aware of myself, writes Geoffrey Madell, and there is no other way to know the "I" than through such direct awareness.

The existence of the self is especially apparent at a biological level. Our brain is a flux of chemical reactions, electrical impulses and constant molecular change. We could not even remember what happened a minute ago if there was no "I" that is stable, enduring and non-physical.

Obviously, each person changes in response to different experiences, develops habits as he or she keeps performing certain acts, and so on. But there is no question it is one single person to whom these changes occur.

In *Our Brains, Our Selves—What a Neurologist's Patients Taught Him About the Brain,* Oxford professor of cognitive neuroscience Masud Husain tells us about what we know about brain disorders and its effect on our sense of self. For instance, split brain surgery has no effect on the unity of the self and Alzheimer's patients retain a sense of self. In his Royal Society Science Prize-winning book, Masud writes:

> "As a procedure to treat chronic, intractable epilepsy … 'disconnection' of the left and right hemispheres [of the brain] from each other can be very effective. … However after surgery, one clear observation was that patients did not show any evidence in their everyday lives of a split self. As far as they were concerned they were the same (unified) person.
>
> Similarly, people who have focal lesions of the brain, such as from a stroke or the excision of a tumour, can show a range of deficits depending upon the location of the brain damage, but there is no evidence that any of them lose their self as a result. They might become different selves as a consequence of their brain damage,

> but they do not lose an understanding of who they are. This is also the case in people who develop slowly progressive neurodegenerative conditions such as Alzheimer's disease. As we saw …, someone like Trish [a patient of the author] can start to lose their episodic memory (recollection of events) because of Alzheimer's, but they do not necessarily lose themselves. They know who they are. Although they may become a different individual, they retain a sense of their previous selves. …
>
> Contrary to John Locke's idea that memory is the glue that keeps a self together, "it has become clear, though, that most patients with amnesia (loss of episodic memory) still retain a sense of themselves, such as personality traits. As Stanley Klein and Cynthia Gangi put it: 'There are no documented cases in which a person … has lost self-knowledge while retaining other components of the self.'"[151]

Lund reminds us that science would not be possible without consciousness and our first-person perspective:

> "The concept of observability does presuppose the concept of an observation. And since the latter concept is at least prima facie a mental one that is informed at some level by our first-person access to our own mental states (an access we have in virtue of our having such states), an analysis of our concept of the physical cannot proceed in the absence of a satisfactory analysis of our concept of mental states and of our first-person access to them. … We would have no conception of the physical and no perceptual awareness of physical objects, direct or indirect, if we had no occurrent mental states—conscious, subjective states to which we have first-person access. Such states have proven to be stubbornly resistant to materialist analysis."[152]

The self, it should be emphasized, is an embodied self, an indivisible unity of physical, intellectual and volitional capacities (although all of these capacities do not necessarily have to be actualized all of the time).

151 Masud Husain, *Our Brains, Our Selves—What a Neurologist's Patients Taught Him About the Brain* (Edinburgh, Great Britain: Canongate Books, 2026), 241-2.

152 David Lund, *The Conscious Self*, op cit., 43-4.

Nevertheless, the self's act of existing is non-physical and therefore independent of the physical.

The One and the Many

"A human being is a single substance, albeit one with both corporeal and incorporeal properties and powers."[153]

—*Edward Feser, Immortal Souls—A Treatise on Human Nature*

"The intellectual and sentient person is the whole biological organism as a focalized unity not a brain. The most conspicuous exercises of intellect are in speech and the hearing of speech, writing, and reading, the forms of communication typical of the human species, exhibiting a unity of motor activity, sentience, and understanding, so that it is not being 'inner' which makes something intellectual or mental.

What we need is a holistic understanding of human beings in which they are conceived of as focalized subjects, the same subject, intellectual, sentient, emotional and bodily at the same time. We could call this a 'mind-involving holism.' And it is this holism that modern materialists conspicuously reject, taking everything conscious to have its only realization in the brain."[154]

—*David Braine, Language and Human Understanding*

In speaking about the self remaining the same through changes in our physical being, it might be thought that we are assuming the Cartesian idea of the human person. But is the "I" simply and solely an immaterial ego? Although Cartesians may claim this to be the case, everyday experience points in a different direction. The "I" is a subject that David Braine aptly describes as a "mind-exercising organism."

Notes Braine, "There is no question of dividing an 'I' or a 'he or she', into parts. The 'I', or 'he or she', presents itself as undivided and indivisible.

153 Edward Feser, *Immortal Souls—A Treatise on Human Nature,* op cit., 505.

154 David Braine, *Language and Human Understanding*, op cit., 306.

And the root of this undividedness and indivisibility lies … in integratedness into the life of a conscious subject."[155]

This approach may seem to needlessly complicate the matter. After all, it is so much easier to have a clean divide between the physical and the non-physical.

But Cartesians pay too high a price for their apparent gain:

The mind-body division of Cartesian dualism conflicts with the obvious unity of the human person just as the physicalist's idea that there are multiple agents in the brain contradicts daily experience.

If the mind is the real "I", how can we talk of the body as a something? What we call the body is unified; its constituents and operations act as part of a single being. But how can the body be a unity if it has no unifier? The body cannot exist as a body if it has no organizational matrix.

The Cartesian talks of a mind as a separate entity from the body which enters the body and uses it as its instrument: but there can be no body if it is not "organized" as a body from the start.

To those who wish to remain true to universal experience, the only available option is the Aristotelian description of organisms.

We should recognize first that every organism is fundamentally an agent. An agent acts or is capable of action and is the unified source and center of all its actions. Hence every living being is an agent.

Beyond the sum of its physics and chemistry is the "center" of all its action, the moving "force" that makes it an agent.

And since these agents are capable of surviving and acting independently, they are therefore autonomous agents.

155 David Braine, *The Human Person—Animal and Spirit,* op. cit., 314-315.

And since their actions are in some fashion driven by goals, every autonomous agent, i.e., every form of life, is fundamentally purpose-driven.

Moreover, agents are both unities and dynamic systems that interact with their environments.

To say that an agent is purpose-driven is to say that all of its activities are driven to meet specific goals whether it be to nourish itself or reproduce—and the agent does this for itself, on its own. It has its own inbuilt dynamism; it is the source and cause of all its actions (growth, maintenance, reproduction).

There are a variety of "actions" of which different classes of agents are capable: ingesting, replicating, moving, responding to stimuli, adapting; being conscious; intending; deciding; understanding; using concepts to articulate and communicate.

The kind of actions that an agent is capable of performing tells us what kind of agent it is.

In studying the hierarchy of agents, we see that there are different kinds of organisms, some capable only of physical acts, others capable of both physical and non-physical acts.

In describing organisms Aristotle used the terminology of the body and its organizational matrix, the "soul." Aristotle held that all life-forms had souls although the kind of soul varied with the kind of being involved. The Aristotelian soul is a principle of organization that gives matter a specific unity, identity, agency and end-directedness whether as plant or animal.

We do not have two substances but one reality, one being—matter that is "informed" or organized by a principle of life into a particular kind of being.

We call it a particular life-form (tree or mammal) depending on the kind of "form" into which the living matter is organized.

The idea of dividing an entity into soul and body makes no sense because we are really talking about different kinds of bodies, each with its own principle of organization.

Different varieties of organisms are different kinds of bodies that are organized, 'formed' or ensouled in different modes. Without its organizational matrix there is no body and without the body there is no organizational matrix. To talk of the body is to recognize its organizational matrix—because the organizational matrix is that which makes something a body, which organizes matter in a specific manner.

In the case of human beings, the intellectual self, the body and the human person come to be in a simultaneous action.

The intellectual self is that which animates, organizes and unifies a conglomerate of matter so that it is now a body and it is the "self-driven" body that constitutes the person.

Without the principle of life and organizational matrix that is the intellectual self, there is no body.

But without the body there is no intellectual self because the human self is intrinsically oriented to the body of which it is the organizational matrix.

Nevertheless, it is the intellectual self that brings a body into being: it has its own act of existing into which it brings the body.

The human subject does perform certain fundamental operations like understanding and willing that are intrinsically non-physical and independent of the physical.

Therefore, its act of existing is not only non-physical but one which does not depend on the body for continued subsistence.

But such an existence without a body is unnatural since a human person is essentially embodied and self-driven.

This Aristotelian picture is true to our experience. Clearly, as we have seen, there is a non-physical dimension to our everyday life. And this means physicalism is a non-starter. But Cartesian dualism doesn't do the job either because my body is integral to who I am.

We are not two entities. Every one of my actions is the action of the intellectual organism that I am and these actions are almost always simultaneously physical and non-physical. We say "almost" because intellectual acts such as an understanding of the arguments laid out here have no physical correlate or structure: it is purely a non-physical act of the person.

Nevertheless it is "my" act: it is me the person who thinks through the arguments just as it is I who goes for a walk using my body.

To be true to our experience is to see things holistically.

This was recognized by Aristotle and his most influential successor, Thomas Aquinas, as also by the modern phenomenologists and (to some extent) such thinkers as Ludwig Wittgenstein. "Aquinas contends that the capacities of a human being must be attributed to the human being itself," writes David Braine. "And not to any of his parts. A human being's soul is the source of his capacities; a human being's body is the material support for such capacities. However a human being is that which has the capacities."[156]

156 David Braine, *The Human Person—Animal and Spirit,* op. cit., 338.

III

"YOU HAVE WITCHCRAFT IN YOUR LIPS"

HENRY V, ACT 5, SCENE 2

"My aim is: to teach you to pass from a piece of disguised nonsense to something that is patent nonsense."[157]

—*Ludwig Wittgenstein, Philosophical Investigations*

"We are now in a position to explain how our vivid sensory experience arises in the sensory cortex of our brains … [and is] embodied in a vast chorus of neural activity…. [W]e can now understand how the infant brain slowly develops a framework of concepts … and how the matured brain deploys that framework almost instantaneously: to recognize similarities, to grasp analogies, and to anticipate both the immediate and the distant future."[158]

—*Paul M. Churchland, The Engine of Reason, The Seat of the Soul*

"You came to this book assuming that the basic units of human cognition are states such as thoughts, beliefs, perceptions, desires, and preferences. … Their universality notwithstanding, these bedrock assumptions are probably mistaken."[159]

—*Paul M. Churchland, The Engine of Reason, The Seat of the Soul*

"I do think that is naughty of Professor Churchland. For one thing, none of it is true. We don't know how the brain deploys its concepts to achieve perception and thought; or how it develops them; or even what concepts are. We don't know how the motor system contrives the integration of the lips, tongue, lungs, velum, and vocal cords in the routine utterance of speech … Nor do we know, to a first glimmer, how a brain (or anything else that is physical) could manage to be a locus of conscious experience. … Nor does Churchland's hyperoptimistic account of the current situation in 'cognitive neuroscience' represent anything like the consensus view among practitioners. … What makes

157 Part 1, § 464.

158 (Cambridge, MA: MIT Press: 1999), 4-7.

159 (Cambridge, MA: MIT Press: 1999), 322.

this naughty of Churchland, and not just ill-advised, is that his book purports to be a popular introduction. … Churchland's book, in fact, is not an overview but a potboiler."[160]

—Jerry Fodor, In Critical Condition

"Behavior is the effect of mental causes, and the paradigm of explanation in cognitive psychology is the attribution of a creature's actions to its beliefs, intentions, desires and other of its `propositional attitudes', which are themselves typically the effects of interactions between its innate endowments and such mental processes as perceiving, remembering and thinking."[161]

—Jerry Fodor and Zenon W Pylyshyn, Minds without Meanings –An Essay on The Content of Concepts

"The cognitive revolution was supposed to create a pedagogical infrastructure that would train researchers to do neuroscience in the light of sophisticated theories of the mind. But, with scattered exceptions, that hasn't happened. Partly that is because even the most sophisticated theories of the mind that we have got are not, by and large, really all that good. But it is also because a lot of mainline neuroscience hasn't done its homework, so the psychology it presupposes is not even the best of a bad lot."[162]

—Jerry Fodor

"Whatever science can show about the mind, it cannot show that there is none." [163]

—William G. Lycan, "A Particularly Compelling Refutation of Eliminative Materialism,"

"Science shows that brain states are connected to states of consciousness but not that the connection is one of identity. Nor does it show that experience is subjectless or, conversely, that an experiencing subject is intrinsic to consciousness. …

What is only rarely acknowledged is that some of the problems facing the materialist appear to be nothing less than insuperable. It seems clear that there can be no satisfactory materialist treatment of either

160 (Cambridge, MA: The MIT Press, 2000), 83.

161 (Cambridge, MA: MIT Press: 2016).

162 *Times Literary Supplement*, May 17 2002.

163 D. M. Johnson & C. E. Erneling (eds.), *The Mind as a Scientific Object: Between Brain and Culture.* (Oxford: Oxford University Press, 2005). http://www.unc.edu/~ujanel/ElimWeb.htm

the qualitative phenomenality of experience or the intentionality of consciousness. ...

A third and equally intractable problem for the materialist comes into view upon considering the issues I treat in this book. If, as I argue, we must acknowledge the existence of a subject of consciousness, the case for ontological materialism is lost."[164]

—*David Lund*

164 David Lund, *The Conscious Self*, op cit., 13-14.

Bewitched

> "Philosophy is a battle against the bewitchment of our intelligence by means of language."[165]
>
> —*Ludwig Wittgenstein, Philosophical Investigations*

PHYSICALISM, BECAUSE IT DENIES self-evident truths, is "disguised nonsense" that can be shown to be "patent nonsense."

Why does physicalism continue to attract adherents despite its nonsensical character? A good part of the answer lies "in the bewitchment of our intelligence by means of language." As Wittgenstein saw it, the way we often use language can create philosophical problems that do not actually exist.

Extrapolations from everyday usage mesmerize us and lead us down rabbit holes to dead-ends. For instance, the madcap notions of dismissing the evident reality of consciousness or the self or of downloading the mind to a digital device derive from the bewitchment of our intelligence by implausible and incoherent thought-experiments, metaphors and dogmas.

This is the second spell we spoke off earlier: Zombies 'R Us, the fantasy that we are zombies without consciousness or intellection.

Once we fall under this spell, the most effective way to break it is to unmask the nonsense underlying it.

To do that we should look back at how we were first drawn into it.

165 §109.

In the initial stages, we were told to reject the hard facts of our immediate experience on the pretext that accepting them on their own terms would jeopardize the completeness of the scientific story. Even more horrifying, they would introduce ghosts or obscure esoteric forces into the self-contained machinery of modern science. We would be thrust back into the Middle Ages.

We were assured that we can safely ignore the data of experience because there are "scientific" theories that can domesticate them suitably. Appearances are deceptive so let's just stick with theory. Getting on this fact-free diet will steer us away from our previous life of sensory excess.

But bewitchment of this kind requires us to keep our eyes wide shut. Colin McGinn, a naturalist who refused to play along with such self-deception, retraces the path taken by physicalism:

> Why did a simple form of materialism gain such traction until quite recently? This is something of a mystery—the mystery of why the mystery was not recognized during this period. …
>
> Not long after [the Victorians] … a new school of thought hit the ground running. It annihilated everything in its wake, in psychology and philosophy. I refer of course to *behaviorism*. The mind was abandoned in favor of the body—the moving reactive body. It was all stimulus and response now. The body is physical: you can see it, touch it, measure it, photograph it. That's all there is (all that science can observe). …
>
> Accordingly, people stopped thinking about the mind from its own perspective: they adopted a third-person point of view. … Psychology became a branch of mechanics, in effect. Pain became pain behavior that can be seen and touched. … The mind proper disappeared from view for decades. Any remnant of the old conception was ruthlessly eliminated (Ryle was a kind of exterminator). …
>
> But eventually the behaviorist creed wore thin: for it neglected the

inner, the internal, the intermediary ("intervening variables"). The black box must have something in it; it wasn't just mush in there. What? The brain, of course. Thus, "central state materialism." This wasn't that much of a departure from behaviorism, as it happens. You can trace muscle contractions back to efferent nerves and their busy neural impulses—aren't they the direct expression of so-called psychological states? …

Scientists could obtain recordings of *brain behavior*. The brain acts, responds, does things: it is a zone of physical behavior. So, we could preserve the spirit of behaviorism while jettisoning its dogmatic focus on the gross body. We could be sophisticated behaviorists—*neurological* behaviorists. We shift focus from the whole body to a vital part of it but preserve the metaphysics of mind presupposed by old-style behaviorism. The next step was obvious enough: identify mental states with brain states, or mental actions with brain actions. …

Materialism is behaviorism internalized. True, brain states seem more alien to the mind than ordinary bodily behavior—not how we normally think—but they are still on the same level as behavior (as atoms are like macroscopic bodies). We have retained the third-person point of view (the point of view from a distance). Hence the occlusion, the abandonment, the suppression of the mental as viewed from the inside. …

But this revised physicalism (the body as the paradigm of the physical) could only maintain its hold for so long. Someone was going to point out that the mind is essentially conscious, that consciousness is real, that it cannot be neglected. The mind came rushing back in its pre-behaviorist form, where it had been left dangling since the late nineteenth century. And with it the old mind-body problem asserted itself—the problem of "concomitance", the problem of "binding." When that happened it was a short step to the rediscovery of the mystery, which had not been advanced one jot. …

Metaphysical behaviorism is dead, external or internal, bodily or cerebral."[166]

166 https://colinmcginn.net/the-deep-problem-of-consciousness/

The FundaMaterialists

So that's how we lost our minds. But there's more to the story.

The game of musical chairs is picking up speed. The musicians are The FundaMaterialists. Every time the music stops, a chair is pulled out. The first to go was named Behaviorism. Its "chairperson" B.F. Skinner scurried away never to be seen again. Then, in quick succession, the Eliminative Materialism and Identity Theory/Central State Materialism folks were put out to pasture. Next to go were the Functionalism and oddly named Anomalous Monism also-rans. Finally, Teams Non-Reductive Materialism, Epiphenomenalism and Emergence, who left nothing but confusion in their wake, were yanked away. Until there were none. But The FundaMaterialists kept playing.

So there we have it. The history of physicalism. The history of an idea whose time has never come.

Of course, physicalism takes on various shapes. We can, in fact, see it as a seven-headed hydra.

The seven heads of the physicalist hydra are our musical chair players. Like the mythical hydra, the physicalist embodiment has proven adept at growing additional heads when one is cut off—hence its multi-headed character. Like the original, the breath and blood of the physicalist hydra are toxic, poisoning thought and distorting reality.

The golden sword that can slay this monster from the deep is a return to the self-evident facts of our experience.

The fundamental claim of the physicalists—uniting all variations of the genus—is that only the physical exists. Only mass and energy exist and all properties are physical. What we describe as consciousness, subjectivity, experience, intentionality and the like are ultimately physical, wholly physical and nothing but physical.

To be sure, there are physicalists and there are physicalists. In the physicalist caste system, the lowest rung on the ladder is occupied by the Behaviorists and the Eliminative and Reductionist Materialists. As we ascend the hierarchy, in quick succession we run into Identity Theorists, Functionalists, Anomalous Monists, Non-Reductive Materialists, Epiphenomenalists and, perched on top, the Emergentists who avoid all conceptual contact with the lower castes.

Now while each theory may have given up the ghost, the ghosts are still around. Apparently, they couldn't rest in peace! The return of the AI Jedi has, in fact, triggered off a feeding frenzy of physicalist vampires with sightings of long-dead delusions. A snapshot of the main players may help us in identifying each species of this underworld.

Species	***Traits***	***AKA***	***Dance form***
Behaviorism	We only observe behavior not "mind": behavior is strictly a response to environmental factors: all behavior is determined by laws of conditioning: consequently, all reference to "mental" causes must be eliminated. What was previously called "mind" is simply a description of observable behavior.	Planet of the Apes	Belly dance
Eliminative Materialism	There are no "inner" events, no such things as beliefs or desires. Everything is reducible entirely to matter in motion.	The Living Dead	Breakdance Headspin
Identity Theory/ Central State Materialism	All mental states are purely and simply neural states, two sides of one coin much as light can also be described as electromagnetic radiation. There is no "mental" reality distinct from the brain. Has two basic variations—type-identity and token-identity.	Physicalists Gone Wild	The Twist

Species	***Traits***	***AKA***	***Dance form***
Functionalism	Embarrassed by Behaviorism and Identity Theory, Functionalism moves away from the question of what makes up mental activity to the issue of the function performed by such activity and its role in a given system. Functionalists deploy the analogy of a computer: the mind is a program realized in the brain just as a program is realized in a computer. Input and output—both entirely physical—are all that matters. Computers do the same kinds of operations as brains so "consciousness" is irrelevant. Only sensory inputs and behavioral outputs are relevant. Focus on function instead of on what happens when you think, feel or see. A "pain" is something that creates an avoidance reaction and a "thought" is an exercise in problem-solving. Neither are private events taking place in a private place. So also all other supposedly mental phenomena. Being conscious means performing these functions. Qualitative aspects of mental events can be safely ignored. For computational functionalists, cognition is the applying of computational processes (algorithms) to representational structures encoded in the brain. Human cognition is information processing, the brain being a computer with rules for working with symbols and structures.	The Matrix	Tap dance

Species	***Traits***	***AKA***	***Dance form***
Non-reductive Materialism	Everything in the world is physical but some items have mental properties not reducible to physical properties. But these mental properties derive entirely from physical laws and properties. This is thanks to "supervenience," a theory that mental properties are dependent on physical properties in a particular way: there is no change in the mental without a change in the physical. The mental supposedly "supervenes" on the physical: "No mental differences without physical differences" is the movement slogan. Adherents refuse to identify specific mental events with specific physical events while claiming the mental is determined by the physical. You can eat your cake and have it too.	Dumb and Dumber	Ballet
Anomalous monism	A form of non-reductive materialism. "Monism" because mental events are identical to physical events. "Anomalous" because there is no correlation between mental properties and brain states or coordination with physical laws. The mental has no role in explaining bodily movements. So there!	Dumb and Dumber To	Walz
Epiphenomenalism	There are non-physical mental events. These are caused by physical events but cannot themselves cause or affect physical events. All traffic is one-way: brain states generate mental states but such mental states cannot affect brain states. Our experience of intentions and choices and of actions driven by beliefs and plans is illusory. This is inertia in all its glory.	The Shining	Mime dance

Species	***Traits***	***AKA***	***Dance form***
Emergentism	The Emergentist admits that novel features sometimes emerge from complex systems. These are novel in the sense that they cannot be reduced to or predicted from the properties of the lower-level components (for instance, water cannot be predicted from the properties of hydrogen and oxygen). When it comes to consciousness, the Emergentist says that psychological properties emerge from certain complex biological systems and these properties cannot be reduced to the biological. But the Emergentist insists that what is experienced as "psychological" is, in essence, physical.	The Revenge of the Nerds	Folk dance

The evolution of Physicalism from its hard-core Behaviorist-Eliminative-Reductionist genesis to soft-core Non-Reductionist/Emergentist mutations is a symptom of the inherent instability of its intellectual infrastructure. Any philosophy that is built on the rejection of both what seems obvious and what seems rationally required cannot long endure.

So it has been with Physicalism.

The Waning of Materialism, cited earlier, outlines some of the intellectual challenges that have made physicalism a game of musical chairs with no winners:

> Historically, materialism was just the reductionist position that mental properties are identical to—and in that sense are nothing but—physical properties...
>
> Over the last fifty or so years, materialism has been challenged by a daunting list of arguments (some inspired by classical arguments from the history of philosophy and others, wholly new) beginning with the Chisholm-Geach-Putnam attack on Behaviorism and fortified by Kripke's attack on the Identity Theory, followed by a host

of others: the multiple realizability argument, the disembodiment argument, the certainty argument, the zombie (or nonconscious automaton) argument, the absent qualia argument, the knowledge argument, the inverted spectrum argument, the argument from the special sciences, the explanatory gap argument, the anti-individualism argument, the self-consciousness argument, the mental causation argument, and many, many more. Taken together, these arguments and sophisticated variations on them constitute a significant prima facie threat to the success of materialism."[167]

167 Robert C. Koons and George Bealer ed. *The Waning of Materialism* (New York: Oxford University Press, 2010), x.

"What Madness Rules in Brainsick Men!"—Thought-Experiments, Metaphors, Dogmas and Ptolemaic Epicycles

Henry VI, Part 1, Act 4, Scene 7

"Being a philosopher, I have a problem for every solution."
—*Robert Zend*

The sane observer, untainted by philosophical promiscuity, may wonder how apparently learned scholars can deny the very facts they rely on to make their case. You can't practice philosophy or science unless you're conscious, a meaning-processor and an enduring self. And yet these are the very facts about themselves they vehemently deny.

Only bewitchment can explain such trains of thought that ride off in all directions at once. This bewitchment is self-inflicted. It derives from the far-fetched thought-experiments, metaphors and dogmas they conjure up from nothing and then apply literally in their discussions. Whenever objections are raised, they construct work-arounds reminiscent of the epicycles created by Ptolemy to preserve his geocentric view of the world.

Thought-experiments

Take thought-experiments.

The 17th century philosopher John Locke pioneered the idea with his fanciful proposal of a prince and a cobbler exchanging minds.

More recently, since the Sixties, fatally flawed thought-experiments have functioned as major arguments in favor of physicalism. We see this in the works of David Wiggins, Derek Parfit, Sydney Shoemaker, Peter Unger, Donald Davidson, Dennett and many others who devised purely speculative experiments built on arbitrary neurological assumptions. It came to be seen later that the experiments were scientifically impossible but by then the damage had been done. The end of supporting physicalism justified the means.

Based only on creative speculation, theorists touted scenarios of different parts of one brain being placed in different bodies. From this entirely imaginary idea, they concluded that one person could thus conceivably be split into two. But if a person could be split into two, then it is simply not possible to say that we are both of those persons. We can only be one of them. But each of the persons would possess the same characteristics and there is nothing to differentiate them. So the original person survives in both. From this the physicalist theorist concluded that the "I" is not something fundamental and personal identity was constituted by collections of experiences.

Kathleen Wilkes points out that "most of the thought experimenters know little (and unfortunately care less) about biology and physiology" and concluded that, "We cannot extract philosophically interesting conclusions from fantastical thought-experiments."[168]

Even worse, most of these proposed thought-experiments were impossible even in theory and therefore irrelevant to the discussion.

> "We are completely ignorant about what would happen if the detachable parts of two half-brains from one head were sewn on to the undetachable parts of the two different brains (death is certainly the most likely outcome), and thus no conclusions relevant to personal identity could be drawn." "Thought-experiments that

168 K. V. Wilkes, *Real People: Personal Identity without Thought Experiments* (Oxford: Clarendon Press, 1999), 19.

> are the product of ignorance simply mislead."[169]

Lukas Meier concludes,

> "Without taking into account biological facts, one is doing philosophy in the realm of science fiction, and it is highly doubtful that conclusions arrived at in this way are trustworthy guides to *our* persistence conditions. Not all questions can be answered from the armchair."[170]

Both the philosopher of science W.V.O. Quine and Thomas Kuhn, author of *The Structure of Scientific Revolutions*, were critical of these stratagems.

> Quine: "The method of science fiction has its uses in philosophy, but (...) I wonder whether the limits of the method are properly heeded. To seek what is 'logically required' for sameness of person under unprecedented circumstances is to suggest that words have some logical force beyond what our past needs have invested them with."[171]

> Kuhn: "If we have to do with a real thought experiment, the empirical data upon which it rests must have been both well-known and generally accepted before the experiment was even conceived."[172]

Unlike scientific experiments, philosophers' thought-experiments do not have to produce hard evidence or pass peer-review and regulatory evaluation.

Metaphor

Metaphor has been another driver of trips to nowhere.

169 Ibid.

170 *Synthese*, 2022, 200-221, https://doi.org/10.1007/s11229-022-03637-7

171 Ibid.

172 Kuhn, T. S., "A function for thought experiments." in *The Essential Tension: Selected Studies in Scientific Tradition and Change* (Chicago: University of Chicago Press, 1978), 241.

Consider, for instance, physicalist Daniel Dennett's own unapologetic admission that his mode of argument is metaphor (as borne out by his books):

> "My explanation of consciousness is far from complete. One might even say that it was just a beginning, but it is a beginning, because it breaks the spell of the enchanted circle of ideas that made explaining consciousness seem impossible. I haven't replaced a metaphorical theory, the Cartesian Theater, with a nonmetaphorical ('literal, scientific') theory. All I have done, really, is to replace one family of metaphors and images with another, trading in the Theater, the Witness, the Central Meaner, the Figment, for Software, Virtual Machines, Multiple Drafts, a Pandemonium of Homunculi. It's just a war of metaphors, you say—but metaphors are not "just" metaphors; metaphors are the tools of thought. No one can think about consciousness without them, so it is important to equip yourself with the best set of tools available. Look what we have built with our tools. Could you have imagined it without them?"[173]

He responded to criticisms not with counter-arguments but analogies and metaphors. Logic has been replaced with rhetoric.

The march of misleading metaphors continues to the present day with hopelessly confused analogies about downloading the mind and the like.

Downloading the mind is conceptually impossible given the immaterial nature of the intellect and the self. But it is fanciful even on a physical level. As its proponents recognize, for this to happen the human brain and each of its states have to be mapped and replicated on a computer. We need what is called whole brain emulation in an artificial setting. We have to simulate, store, retrieve and process the biological brain's 100 trillion connections in an artificial brain.

173 Daniel Dennett, *Consciousness Explained* (New York: Little, Brown and Company, 1991), 455.

According to Miguel Nicolelis, a neuroscientist at Duke, "The brain is not computable and no engineering can reproduce it."[174]

Damian Pang points out that "There is an even bigger challenge: We still have no idea how consciousness works. Even if we managed to upload all the information inside our brains onto a computer, there is no clear evidence that that information alone would be sufficient to produce consciousness."[175]

The eliminativist Paul Churchland provides a textbook example of erroneous extrapolation—using words which make sense in one domain and applying it an entirely different sphere without any effort to demonstrate the similarity.

As Ed Feser writes, Churchland

> "tells us that, contrary to what philosophers have supposed historically, the 'fundamental unit of cognition' is not the judgment, with its susceptibility of truth or falsity and its logical relation to other judgments, but rather 'the *activation pattern* across a proprietary *population* of neurons.' Nor does 'theoretical understanding' consist primarily in the grasp of sentences or propositions, but rather in 'an *unfolding sequence of activation-vectors* within the brain.' Nor does knowledge fundamentally involve justified true belief. Rather, a 'conceptual framework' turns out to be 'a hierarchically structured, high-dimensional activation space,' and 'a perceptual representation' turns out to be 'a 106-element neuronal activation vector.' And Churchland tells us that while such neurological 'representational vectors ... can have, or lack, sundry representational virtues,' they 'are not the sorts of things to which the notion of Tarskian truth even applies.'
>
> "Now, little or nothing in the way of argument is actually given by Churchland for any of these claims. A general materialism is

174 https://www.technologyreview.com/2013/02/18/180012/the-brain-is-not-computable/

175 https://www.psychologytoday.com/us/blog/consciousness-and-beyond/202402/can-we-upload-our-minds-to-a-computer#:~:text=But%20there%20is%20an%20even,be%20sufficient%20to%20produce%20consciousness.

> simply taken for granted, and it is insinuated that since processes of the sort Churchland describes are the ones neuroscientists are discovering within the brain, they must be what cognition essentially consists in. To his credit, Churchland sees that the properties in terms of which thought is typically characterized—propositional content, truth and falsity, logical inter-relationships, and so forth—simply cannot intelligibly be applied to the brute physiological processes he is interested in. But, in that case, what reason can there be to characterize such processes as embodying 'cognition,' 'understanding 'knowledge,' or the having of a 'conceptual framework' in the first place? When stripped of propositional content, truth or falsity, logical connections, and the like, how does a pattern of neural activity constitute a 'cognition' any more than the flexing of a tendon or the secretion of bile constitutes a cognition? In fact, Churchland is simply equivocating, using terms like 'cognition,' 'concept,' etc. in a novel way, as stand-ins for physiological description. He is in no way *explaining* cognition in terms of physiology. He is instead simply *ignoring* (or even *eliminating*) cognition altogether and talking about physiology instead, using the vocabulary of cognition but in a way that is mostly contrary to its usual sense."[176]

Jerry Fodor explains that

> "Churchland is in love with dimensions, vectors and prototypes. His idea is to do for concepts at large what hue and saturation allow you to do for colors: locate them in a 'multi-dimensional vector space' and then look for correlations between the vector values. ... So concepts are a region of cognitive dimensions; *that's* the breakthrough. ... Saying that we conceptualize things as regions in a multidimensional space is saying no more than we conceptualize things. The appearance of progress is merely rhetorical."[177]

---

176 Edward Feser, *Immortal Souls—A Treatise on Human Nature* (Neunkirchen-Seelscheid, Germany: Editions Scholasticae, 2024), 329-330.

177 Jerry Fodor, *In Critical Condition* (Cambridge, MA: The MIT Press, 2000), 88.

While granting the value of metaphors, Michael Pollan also points to the risk:

> "Metaphors can be powerful tools for thinking, as long as we don't forget that they are metaphors—imperfect or partial analogies likening one thing to another. The differences between the two things are as important as the similarities, but these differences seem to have gotten lost in the enthusiasm surrounding AI. As the biologist Richard Lewontin once said, 'The price of metaphor is eternal vigilance.' … The whole field of AI appears to have let down its guard on this one."[178]

Dogma

Then there is the influence of dogma.

Any review of the material in discussions on the mind will show that the goal of many physicalists is not to learn about mind or consciousness but to preserve physicalism at all costs.

Again Dennett is brutally honest:

> "Dualism is to be avoided at all costs. It is not that I think I can give a knock-down proof that dualism, in all its forms, is false or incoherent, but that, given the way dualism wallows in mystery, accepting dualism is giving up."[179]

It is not the evidence that matters but the elimination of rivals to the reigning world order.

Workarounds

And this leads to the need for workarounds.

178 Michael Pollan, *A World Appears: A Journey into Consciousness* (New York: Penguin Press. 2026), 103.

179 Daniel Dennett, *Consciousness Explained.*

If there is any evidence that seems to conflict with physicalism—and there is plenty of that as we have seen—the standard response is to change the current version of physicalism with a reinvented one. The king is dead. Long live the king.

Such is the strategy of proponents of a scientific paradigm that is on its last legs. The most famous example of holding on to a doomed paradigm with ad hoc workarounds was the Ptolemaic epicycle.

When new astronomical evidence threatened Ptolemy's second century geocentric view of the universe, the response was to create ad hoc workarounds to the theory (suggesting, for example, that there were smaller circular paths for the planets called epicycles). Eventually, the accumulation of evidence in favor of the sun being the center of the solar system forced a change of paradigm.

Brain Fog

We began with the reversal of reality running through recent commentaries on AIs and humans: we are deprived of consciousness and mind (courtesy of the old physicalists) but our machines are endowed with sentience and understanding (courtesy of the new physicalists).

What is taken away with one hand (from us) is given with the other (to our creations).

As discussed, misplaced metaphors of "information"-processing, minds-as-software and brains-as-hardware contributed to this tragi-comedy. Call it brain fog.

Another insidious notion dragged us further down: the prophetic proclamation that our brains are syntax machines posing as semantic machines.

The idea seemed especially suited for the AI age because generative AI truly is a syntax machine which some of its users see as a semantic machine.

That didn't seem too hard to believe if we also regarded our brains as semantic poseurs built purely and simply on syntax.

The classic formulation of this monstrosity of a misconception came from Dennett:

> "Brains … are supposed to be *semantic engines*. What brains are *made of* is kazillions of molecular pieces that interact according to the strict laws of chemistry and physics, responding to shapes and

> forces; brains, in other words, are in fact only *syntactic engines*."[180]

He had no evidence, of course, to back up this bizarre view: only a medley of misleading metaphors.

The charade could not last. It was clinically dissected and disposed of by David Bentley Hart:

> "Functionalism is the fundamentally incoherent notion that the human brain is what Daniel Dennett calls a "syntactic engine", which over the ages evolution has rendered able to function as a "semantic engine" …
>
> The governing maxim of functionalism is that, once a proper syntax is established in the neurophysiology of the brain, the semantics of thought will follow; once the syntactic engine begins running its impersonal algorithms, the semantic engine will eventually emerge or supervene. What we call "thought" is allegedly a merely functional, irreducibly physical system for processing data into behaviour. It is, so to speak, software—coding—and nothing more. …
>
> This is nothing but a farrago of vacuous metaphors. Functionalism tells us that a system of physical "switches" or operations can generate a syntax of functions, which in turn generates a semantics of thought, which in turn produces the reality (or illusion) of private consciousness and intrinsic intention. Yet none of this resembles anything that a computer actually does, and certainly none of it is what a brain would do if *it* were a computer. Neither computers nor brains are either syntactic or semantic engines—in fact, neither syntactic nor semantic engines exist, or possibly could. Syntax and semantics exist only as intentional structures, inalienably, in a hermeneutical rather than physical space, and then only as inseparable aspects of an already existing semiotic system. Syntax has no existence prior to or apart from semantics and symbolic thought, and none of these has any existence except within the intentional

180 Daniel Dennett, *Intuition Pumps and Other Tools for Thinking* (New York: W.W. Norton, 2013), 178.

activity of a living mind."[181]

181 David Bentley Hart, "The pool of Narcissus: Reflections on Artificial Intelligence" https://www.abc.net.au/religion/david-bentley-hart-narcissus-reflections-on-ai/102812590

How We Got Here—A Fact-Free Diet

We spoke of the need for the next paradigm-shift, an industry-wide shift away from physicalism.

But what's standing in the way of this shift?

How long will the "sound and fury signifying nothing" continue?

In some ways, the new aura of AI has managed to reverse the death-spiral of FundaMaterialism.

The New Animism of today's talkative bots is the latest entrant in the FundaMaterialist musical chair contest.

But, more fundamentally, what keeps the game going in the teeth of all the counter-evidence is an intellectual pathology with deep-rooted causes.

How else can we explain the fact that one famous philosopher (Daniel Dennett) made his name with the claim that consciousness is an illusion, a user illusion of the brain. In other words, appearances notwithstanding, we are not conscious. ("Human consciousness … says Dennett, is 'the brain's 'user illusion' of itself.'"[182])

Another (Paul Churchland) is famous for his assertion that beliefs, desires and intentions simply don't exist. Yes, nobody has believed or desired anything—ever.

Yet other philosophers cheerfully proclaim that they don't exist.

182 https://www.bbc.com/news/science-environment-39482345

Books, seminars, courses, podcasts have been built around these insane ideas.

How could anyone come up with such ludicrous claims, you might ask, let alone attract adoring audiences?

We remember, of course, that the philosopher Zeno said that motion is impossible. George Berkeley held that things exist only as ideas in our mind. Both views—as well as a procession of other preposterous propositions—were and still are taken seriously by the literate public.

We cannot underestimate the gullibility of the many even if it means losing their minds.

Yet, if we want to keep our sanity, we need to stay true to our experience. And we know that physicalism won't "cut it" simply from the very fact that the physicalists have to constantly move from one theory to another.

Take non-reductive materialism. It is not essentially different from the plain old materialism that more sophisticated physicalists find embarrassing. If you are a materialist but proclaim also that you are not a reductive materialist, you seem to be saying that the mental cannot (absurdly) be reduced entirely to the material. The obvious question is: how you can say this while still assuring us that you are a materialist? Jaegwon Kim, a physicalist, has argued for many years that non-reductive materialists ultimately have no choice but to admit that they are reductive materialists. This argument has been further developed by Timothy O'Connor and John Ross Churchill by applying the principle of causal powers: if all the mental "work" is done by material processes, why suggest that there is something over and above the material involved?

Is it the evidence that keeps the physicalist locked into their views? Clearly not, as several physicalists themselves have said. William Lycan, a materialist for many decades, admitted:

> "Arguments for materialism are few. Tyler Burge and others have maintained that the naturalistic picture of the world is more like a political or religious ideology than like a position well-supported by evidence, and that materialism is an article of faith based on the worship of science. That is an overstatement. But it is true that the original 20th-century materialists felt no need to defend materialism itself. Ryle gave no such argument that I can recall; he only inveighed against the particularly Cartesian 'dogma of the Ghost in the Machine'. Ullin Place, founder of the Identity Theory, gave none; he was originally a Behaviourist who bravely and honestly acknowledged that introspectible occurrent sensations were a problem for Behaviourism and, while making an exception for them, tried to account for them within the materialist framework, but without defending the need to do so.
>
> ...
>
> I mean to have shown here that although Cartesian dualism faces some serious objections, that does not distinguish it from other philosophical theories, and the objections are not an order of magnitude worse than those confronting materialism in particular. There remain the implausibilities required by the Cartesian view; but bare claim of implausibility is not argument. Nor have we seen any good argument for materialism. The dialectical upshot is that, on points, and going just by actual arguments as opposed to appeals to decency and what good guys believe, materialism is not significantly better supported than dualism."[183]

David Papineaux, one of today's prominent physicalists, confesses that "something stops us really believing the materialist identification of mind with brain, even those of us who officially profess materialism."

183 William G. Lycan (2009), "Giving Dualism its Due", *Australasian Journal of Philosophy*, 87:4, 551-563, DOI: 10.1080/00048400802340642

The only effective remedy for this, he writes, is not an improved theory but philosophical "therapy."[184]

Fodor highlighted the extremely tenuous nature of what can be concluded from studies of the brain. About contemporary neuroscience he observes that leading brain scientists cannot keep up with their own latest work let alone cognitive science theories of the mind.

> "Keeping up both with brain science and the fashions in cognitive science must be a practical impossibility; all the more so since the fashions in cognitive science are famously labile. The consequences have been disconcerting. … often enough, the models of the brain that brain science is building are designed to implement a cognitive psychology that nobody with any sense has believed for decades. And the extent of the mismatch tends to increase, as one works one's way inward from relatively peripheral cognitive processes like perception to relatively central ones like learning and reasoning. So our brain science is often least convincing in respect of just those aspects of cognitive processes that we would most like to understand."[185]

The stickiness of the physicalist pathology derives from four underlying thought-patterns:

> Clearly there is a connection between processes in the brain and our mental activity and so it makes sense to identify the mental with the neurological.
>
> If we entertain the idea of any non-physical process or entity, we would be giving up science and reason and surrendering to superstition and invoking mystical and occult forces.
>
> The introduction of any non-physical process would violate the law of conservation of mass and energy which demands

184 David Papineau, *Thinking About Consciousness*, (Oxford: Clarendon Press, 2002), 94, 4.

185 *Times Literary Supplement*, May 17 2002.

> that the total mass and energy of a system has to remain constant. This is a definitive ground for rejecting any non-physical force of any kind.
>
> Finally, we have the insoluble interaction problem. How could a non-physical process interact with physical processes? There is no way to show that this is possible.

What is remarkable about these kinds of physicalist critiques is that they neither deny nor address conscious and cognitive experience. They simply adduce extraneous reasons for rejecting them as realities in their own right. For instance, as we will see, Papineau is worried about them infringing on the completeness of physics. Dennett is concerned that the slightest concession will bring back the dreaded specter of Cartesianism. No evidence that is not measurable is admissible because the physicalist framework only allows physical facts.

Each one of the physicalist straitjackets can be easily stripped away.

Of course, there is a connection between the mental and the neurological. But there is an undeniable difference of kind between our ruminations on the meaning of life and the neural firings accompanying these ruminations. But correlation is not identification. There is no evidence whatsoever that the brain "causes" these ruminations let alone that it can be identified with them. All we know is that the brain serves as a transmission medium for our thoughts just as a cell phone serves as a vehicle for our conversations.

Neal Grossman reminds us that

> "William James (1898) showed, more than a hundred years ago, that (1) the most that the facts of neurology can establish is a correlation between mental states and brain states and (2) correlation is not causation. The data of neuroscience will always be neutral with respect to the hypotheses of (1) causation or materialism and (2) what James called "transmission," the hypothesis that the brain

> merely transmits an already existing consciousness into the particular form that is us. Neuroscience cannot in principle distinguish between these two hypotheses."[186]

Frank Dilley points out that an investigator "can infer from what is going on in someone's brain what mental state that person is experiencing, but she cannot thereby capture that mental state itself. She could infer from the state of the brain that someone is feeling pain, but she will not thereby know *what it is like* for that person to feel pain." In fact she "cannot even experience *her own mental states* by observing her brain."[187] McGinn, we saw earlier, pointed out that since conscious states "are non-spatial they are in principle unperceivable."

And, as we have seen, the human self cannot be located in any part of the brain or the brain as a whole.

On the second claim, the fear that we will be giving up on science is simply silly. It is consciousness and cognition that enabled us to develop and pursue the entire scientific enterprise. The great theories of science were not generated by mindless material processes. Science itself bears witness to its progenitors being rational, conscious creatures capable of conceptual thought and insight. They are the ones who developed a framework of measuring quantities which is what we mean by science. They did not also stipulate that measurable quantities are the only things that exist.

Papineau explicitly admits that science does not require the elimination of the non-physical. In *The Rise of Physicalism*, he argues that

> "without the completeness of physics, there is no compelling reason to identify the mind with the brain. But once the completeness of physics became part of established science, scientifically informed philosophers realized that this crucial premise could be slotted into the various alternative versions of the causal argument

186 *Journal of Near-Death Studies*, March 31, 2008, 238.

187 *International Journal for Philosophy of Religion*, 55:135–153, 2004.

> for physicalism. … Of course, as with all empirical matters, there is nothing certain here. *There is no knock-down argument for the completeness of physics* [emphasis added]. You could in principle accept the rest of modern physical theory, and yet continue to insist on special mental forces, which operate in as yet undetected ways in the interstices of intelligent brains."[188]

Which takes us to the conservation of mass-energy question. Papineau's strategy is to argue that modern science holds that all physical events are completely explained by physical factors. To introduce anything non-physical is to violate this principle of the completeness of physical explanation. To say that an immaterial intellect can "cause" physical events to take place, according to this argument, is to defy the principle of the conservation of energy.

But does consciousness violate the law of conservation of energy? Dilley notes that "mind is not an energy system, and mind does not work on the physical world by exerting energy on it but works by influencing the distribution of energy within the physical world."[189]

On Papineau's concern that immaterial acts accompanying the material violate physical law, E.J. Lowe writes:

> "Even if one has identified all the physical causes of a certain physical event within a certain spacetime region—for instance, even if one has identified all the neural events causally responsible for a certain bodily movement—this doesn't preclude the possibility that the existence of a non-physical (mental) event or state, such as a person's belief or desire or intention, might serve to explain why that movement is non-coincidental, in a way in which the purely physical causal history of that movement does not …. The non-physical part of the explanation need not deny anything which has been discovered about the identity of the physical causes and their purely physical causal relations and is in this sense perfectly compatible with the purely physical part of the

188 David Papineau, "The Rise of Physicalism" in Carl Gillett and Barry Loewer ed. *Physicalism and its Discontents* (Cambridge University Press, 2001).

189 *International Journal for Philosophy of Religion*, 55:135–153, 2004.

explanation."[190]

Lowe finds Papineau's notion that conscious states can somehow be identified with physical states unintelligible:

> "I cannot at all understand what it would mean to say that the state of consciously thinking of Paris just is a 'physical' state. This is because a physical state, by its very nature, is a state whose possession by a thing requires that thing to occupy some part of space ... But my consciously thinking of Paris has no spatial implications of this sort whatsoever, so far as I can see (cf. McGinn, 1995). In fact, the identity-conditions of mental states are simply quite unlike those of physical states... And consequently the thesis that mental states 'just are' (identical with) physical states is simply unintelligible."[191]

On the interaction problem, we should note that this is a problem for both physicalists and Cartesian dualists.

In both cases, the unity of the human person has been split up. They are two sides of one coin.

As we saw, Descartes split the human person into two independent substances, the body being made up of interacting parts governed by physical laws and the soul as an entity capable only of rational thought that is inserted into the body. How such different substances can interact is the problem.

Where the Cartesian dualists have two independent parts, the physicalists have created what is rightly called a pandemonium theory where each human person is made up of multiple competing agents in the brain. In rejecting the unitary self they have created a multitude of selfs. This is Multiple Personality Disorder on steroids. As David Braine describes it,

190 E.J. Lowe, "Self, Agency And Mental Causation" in Benjamin Libet, Anthony Freeman and Keith Sutherland eds. *The Volitional Brain: Towards a Neuroscience of Freewill* (Exeter, UK: Imprint Academic, 1999), 232.

191 Ibid., 227-8.

> "The philosopher Dennett has followed Marvin Minsky and many others in identifying the workings of the mind with the workings of the brain. This brain is represented as composed of a multiplicity of systems, each with its own genealogy and history; metaphorically these systems are 'agents' forming a society, so that the history of each becomes in effect a biography in its own right, these "agents" being like the homunculi or demons spoken of by other AI theorists. In Dennett's account it is as if each system or 'agent' produces a draft text of what might be true in the view of the human being as a whole. …
>
> [This] 'pandemonium theory' has to find a way a way of establishing some hierarchy or rule among the 'demons'. To avoid the chaos resulting from all the 'systems,' 'demons,' or 'agents' putting their draft reports forward at the same time, a certain hierarchy has to emerge among the different drafts."

The physicalists have found it impossible to create any order out of this chaos—or pandemonium as they themselves rightly describe it. Neither is their "pandemonium" theory true to human experience. Braine highlights the contrast:

> "Dennett ends up in a denial of the reality of the 'self' because [of] his whole method of approach … He is looking for the self in a place where it does not exist. For, in truth, the self is nothing other than the human person, by nature a bodily, sentient, intellectual organism belonging to a certain biological species."[192]

So the interaction problem affects both Cartesian and physicalist accounts. What is worse, neither account is compatible with our own experience of being unified agents.

Only Aristotelian holism is true to experience. We are agents with physical and non-physical properties and an organizational matrix that unifies us—the intellectual, sensory self. Only this can explain our everyday experience.

---

192 David Braine, *Language and Human Understanding* (Washington D.C.: CUA Press, 2014), 298, 301, 345.

But is it possible to definitively settle the debate with the various physicalisms? It soon becomes clear that the methodology we adopt in addressing the question of physicalism will determine the kind of answer we give ourselves.

If we decide to only go by methods and tools designed to monitor and measure physical quantities, we will never "find" anything non-physical. If we consider such features of our experience as consciousness and intentionality on their own terms—as phenomena that are realities in their own right—we will begin to make progress in our understanding of their nature and provenance.

By and large, the hard-core physicalists adopt the first approach of keeping out anything intangible and therefore arrive at the answers with which they started. "Hard-core" here includes the Behaviorists, the Eliminative Materialists, the Functionalists and, depending on the time of day, the Identity Theorists.

Being conscious, seeing meaning, having a first-person perspective are experiences and realities that can only be known and described by those who are actually conscious, thinking and describable as "I"s.

Neither the most learned scientists nor the most astute philosophers have any greater competence to speak about these realities than any person who is conscious, thinking or an I. Actually such thinkers often fail to grasp the astounding nature of these realities because they retreat behind the tools and jargon of their trade instead of paying attention to their own experience.

They move around in the world of quantum fields while ignoring the very world of seeing and touching, feeling and hearing, conceptualizing and intending that enables them to explore quantum fields. Awareness is the starting point and the end-point and those who do not grasp this simply forfeit their right to speak about it.

Paradoxically, we have some relevant advice here from Sir Alfred Ayer (known also as A.J. Ayer) who launched Logical Positivism in the English-speaking world with his book *Language, Truth and Logic*. Logical Positivism was the view that only what is verifiable by science is real—a view that went out of vogue a long time ago but is still held by at least some scientists.

Sir Alfred was a participant in our conference on AI and the mind. It is surely significant that, in a discussion with me, even he, a champion of the scientific method, recognized the impossibility of identifying the mental with the physical.

> "The mental is distinct from the material in the sense that I don't see a sufficient cause for identifying them. The mental is very simple. My seeing such and such, hearing such and such, or feeling such emotions, or having such and such a sensation, or whatever, [cannot be identified] with neural processes. I think there's a causal dependency but don't see any grounds for there being an identity. I criticize Ryle [Gilbert Ryle, author of *The Concept of Mind*]. I did in fact argue that he hadn't made out his case. I think it is a marvelous book because I think it is stylistically brilliant. But I don't think he exorcises the ghost and I tried to show exactly why I didn't think that."[193]

193 Sir Alfred Ayer in Roy Varghese, ed. *Great Thinkers on Great Questions* (Oxford: OneWorld Publications, 1998), 49.

“The Comedy of Errors”—Physicalists vs. Physicalists

Physicalists deny the hard facts of experience: conscious experience; thinking in concepts that are not simply the product of neuronal firings; and a self that unifies our experience and thought.

Remarkably, physicalists themselves have called out the absurdity inherent in these rejections in debates with fellow physicalists.

Consider these critiques of the behaviorism of B.F. Skinner, the materialism of David Papineau, the functionalism of Daniel Dennett and then of other forms of physicalism.

Brand Blanshard in a debate with behaviorist B.F. Skinner:

> “It is one of the paradoxes about behaviorists that they first tell us that pains and thoughts are just physical movements in space, and then when we draw the conclusion that we should be able to see them like other such movements, they draw back in dismay. Surely they should either give up the theory that these processes are physical movements—that is, give up behaviorism—or else go courageously forward to the view that we may hope, with a new electronic microscope, to see someone’s toothache or concept of liberty lurking or scurrying about in his head. This the behaviorist feels, with the rest of us, to be absurd. On his premises, I do not see why. … Professor Skinner does deny that pains and thoughts can be seen, and, on that ground, apparently, questions whether there really are such things. … [But if a behaviorist] tells me that my consciousness of an intense pain is an illusion, I can only say, No, thank you; if that is science, I prefer to stay with common

sense or (heaven help me) philosophy."[194]

Ted Honderich in a debate with David Papineau:

> "David, as I say, is a real materialist and a real materialist, for present purposes, is somebody who thinks that a mental episode has only neural properties, no others. And it seems to me that that is dead mistaken, because of something I want to call the 'wholly resilient proposition'. The proposition that never lies down for long. It always gets up and fights again. It always overtakes more people than are ever convinced by philosophers. And the wholly resilient proposition is that the *properties* of such conscious events as your now feeling something, your now thinking of what I'm saying—the properties of conscious events aren't neural ones. They're not matters of transmitter substances and electrical potentials. That is the wholly resilient proposition. And it seems to me that it defeats absolutely the real materialism that David is strongly inclined to hold.
>
> And finally there's the last criterion for a good account of consciousness and that's the wholly resilient proposition. The wholly resilient proposition is that *none* of us really believes—not even *David* although he tries it on at the end of his book—that thinking or feeling, or the experience of seeing, has only neural properties. Any decent account of consciousness has to satisfy that criterion."[195]

John Searle in a debate with Daniel Dennett:

> "In my account of consciousness I start with the data; Dennett denies the existence of the data. To put it as clearly as I can: in his book, *Consciousness Explained*, Dennett denies the existence of consciousness. He continues to use the word, but he means something different by it. For him, it refers only to third-person phenomena, not to the first-person conscious feelings and experiences we all have. …

---

194 *Philosophy and Phenomenological Research*, 27:3, March 1967, 317-337.

195 https://philosophynow.org/issues/29/Introducing_Consciousness

I think most readers, when first told this, would assume that I must be misunderstanding him. Surely no sane person could deny the existence of feelings. But in his reply he makes it clear that I have understood him exactly. He says, "How could anyone deny that!? Just watch..."

How does he think he can, so to speak, get away with this? At this point in the argument his letter misrepresents the nature of the issues. He writes that the disagreement between us is about rival "intuitions," that it is between my "time-tested intuitions" defending "traditional opinion" against his more up-to-date intuitions, and that he and I "have a deep disagreement about how to study the mind." But the disagreement is not about intuitions and it is not about how to study the mind. It is not about methodology. It is about the existence of the object of study in the first place. ...

The very existence of my conscious states is not similarly a matter for my intuitions. The refutable intuitions I mentioned require a distinction between how things seem to me and how they really are, a distinction between appearance and reality. But where the existence of conscious states is concerned, you can't make the distinction between appearance and reality, *because the existence of the appearance is the reality in question*. If it consciously seems to me that I am conscious, then I am conscious. It is not a matter of "intuitions," of something I feel inclined to say. Nor is it a matter of methodology. Rather it is just a plain fact about me—and every other normal human being—that we have sensations and other sorts of conscious states.

Now what am I to do, as a reviewer, in the face of what appears to be an obvious and self-refuting falsehood? Should I pinch the author to remind him that he is conscious? Or should I pinch myself and report the results in more detail? The method I adopted in my review was to try to diagnose what philosophical assumptions lead Dennett to deny the existence of conscious states, and as far as I can tell from his letter he has no objection to my diagnosis. He thinks the conclusion that there are no conscious states follows from two axioms that he holds explicitly, the objectivity of science and verificationism. These are, first, that science uses objective or third-person methods, and second, that nothing exists which cannot be verified by scientific methods so construed. I argued at some length in my review that the objectivity of science does not have the consequence he thinks it does. The *epistemic* objectivity of method does not preclude *ontological* subjectivity of subject matter. To state this in less fancy jargon: the fact that many people have back pains, for example, is an objective fact of medical science. The existence of these pains is not a matter of anyone's opinions or attitudes. But the mode of existence of the pains themselves is subjective. They exist only as felt by human subjects. In short the only formal argument I can find in his book for the denial of consciousness rests on a fallacy. He says nothing in his letter to respond to my argument."[196]

Galen Strawson on Dennett:

"Dennett made the great mistake of his philosophical generation. He was sure (just like Descartes, whom he reviled) that we know enough about the nature of the physical to know that consciousness can't be physical. He made the mistake in the face of all the evidence—the evidence of science—that the stuff of the world is profoundly strange, far stranger, it seems, than we can ever hope to understand. Dennett was, in this respect, a fanatic. Religious fanatics believe in the existence of something for which there is no evidence. Dennett went further: he denied the existence of something whose existence is certain. (If he is right, there has never been any pain or suffering or joy; not really.)"[197]

Steven Pinker on Dennett:

Dennett's book "should have been called *Consciousness Explained Away* instead of *Consciousness Explained.* The reason the book is in some way unsatisfying is that there's another aspect of the problem of consciousness for which no one has yet come up with a satisfactory explanation: why there's a clear intuitive difference between one organism that feels pain and another organism that acts as if

196 https://www.nybooks.com/articles/1995/12/21/the-mystery-of-consciousness-an-exchange/

197 https://www.lrb.co.uk/the-paper/v46/n12/anil-gomes/tillosophy

it feels pain but doesn't really feel it."[198]

William Lycan on Eliminative Materialism:

> "Eliminative Materialism is materialism or physicalism plus the distinctive and truly radical thesis that there have never occurred any sensations; no one has ever experienced a sensation. .... plus the claim that no creature has ever had a belief, desire, intention, hope, wish or the like."

Lycan, himself a physicalist, points to some of the arguments adduced by physicalists themselves in arguing against Eliminative Materialism:

> "We know there are propositional attitudes because we introspect them in ourselves. The posited attitudes are indispensable to prediction, reasoning, deliberation and understanding, and/or to the capturing of important macroscopic generalizations, and/or to various less cognitive pursuits."
>
> "'Cognitive suicide' arguments show that Eliminativism is ... self-refuting."[199]

Jerry Fodor was at one and the same time the most prominent proponent and critic of the functionalist model of the mind in which the mind is seen as a repository of representations that we use to make systematic computations. In *The Mind Doesn't Work That Way*, Fodor reached a stunning conclusion:

> "The last forty or fifty years have demonstrated pretty clearly that there are aspects of higher mental processes into which the current armamentarium of computational models, theories, and experimental techniques offers vanishingly little insight. ...
>
> What our cognitive science has done so far is mostly to throw some light on how much dark there is. So far, what our cognitive science

198 John Brockman, *The Third Culture* (New York: Simon & Schuster, 1995), 195.

199 William G. Lycan, "A Particularly Compelling Refutation of Eliminative Materialism," in D. M. Johnson & C. E. Erneling (eds.), *The Mind as a Scientific Object: Between Brain and Culture.* (Oxford: Oxford University Press, 2005). http://www.unc.edu/~ujanel/ElimWeb.htm

has found out about the mind is mostly that we don't know how it works."[200]

200 Jerry Fodor, *The Mind Doesn't Work That Way: The Scope and Limits of Computational Psychology* (Cambridge, MA: MIT Press, 2001), 2, 100.

Killing YourSelf

THE SUBJECTIVE NATURE of experiences results from the fact that they are experiences of a subject. You are a subject of consciousness because of certain intrinsic properties not extrinsic properties like dependence on the brain. Moreover, "in first-person terms, there can be no answer to the question as to what it is for some item in the centerless material order to be *me*."[201] No physicalist account can explain a subject of conscious experiences, the self.

But determined physicalists will not let self-evident truths and hard facts of experience get in their way. A favorite escape route is to call the self an illusion (created by whom we might ask!), a trick the brain plays on itself (notice how "self" creeps back in). Another older approach is to do some "self-searching" and then triumphantly announce that no self was located in one's thoughts and perceptions (again we ask: who performed the search?).

Thought-experiments of slicing brains in half and placing them in different skulls to (allegedly) create two selves and cases of Dissociative Identity Disorder (previously known as Multiple Personality Disorder) are then offered up as refutations of the idea of a single enduring self. But these arguments no longer hold any force.

Commissurotomy (split-brain) surgery severing the fibers connecting the left and right hemispheres of the brain, is a well-known surgical procedure. But Roger Sperry, the Nobel Prize winner who pioneered

201 David Lund, *The Conscious Self*, op cit., 14.

this procedure, made it clear that it had no bearing on the unity of the self:

> "Instead of concluding ... that the normal intact brain must have two separate, left and right minds (harboring, in effect, two separate conscious selves), I could think of conscious experience in the intact brain as an overriding unified entity that normally is "different from and more than" the sum of the conscious experience of the two separate hemispheres. It followed, further, that the unified subjective intent must causally program the patterns of neuronal firing within each hemisphere without interfering with the physical or chemical laws of the neuronal processing at physiological levels."[202]

As for the philosophers' fanciful thought-experiments of splitting selves, we saw that these have been shown to be scientifically implausible and in some cases theoretically impossible—and therefore irrelevant to the discussion.

What about Dissociative Identity Disorder (formerly known as Multiple Personality Disorder)? DID is now regarded a treatable condition of a single self in turmoil—not of different selves in the same body. Even if one accepts DID as a real condition, it does not suggest the absence of an underlying self.

In *First Person Plural: Multiple Personality and the Philosophy of Mind*, Stephen Braude points out that the colonial view of the self (where the self is regarded as a colony of lower-order selves) springs from 19th century psychological ideas of associationism. This view is based on the "Humpty-Dumpty fallacy," the idea that because Humpty Dumpty broke into 40 pieces when he fell, he was therefore originally made up of these 40 pieces. Actually the multiplicity points to an underlying unity of mind. The various interacting traits require "the hypothesis of

202 Roger W. Sperry, "Consciousness, Personal Identity and the Divided Brain", *Neuropsychologia*, 1984;22(6):661-73. (doi: 10.1016/0028-3932(84)90093-9.)

an underlying synthesizing subject who simply evolves into a multiple as a complex and creative response to various life situations."[203]

Braude says that the

> "dissociated states in some sense belong to the person, even though they may be outside conscious awareness; and that dissociated material is thus in principle accessible to consciousness, given the proper means of accessing it." He holds that a unifying self or ego is a precondition for the existence of the alters and concludes that we "need not deny either the reality and functional distinctness of alters or the reality and functional complexity of the underlying subject to whom the entire repertoire of abilities belongs." He adds, "We need to posit something like an underlying and unifying Kantian ego to explain" the alters or "apperceptive centers" displayed in cases of DID."[204]

DID and split-brains are not the only mental disorders that affect the functioning of the human person. Numerous other conditions ranging from amnesia to Alzheimer's severely affect brain functions. But the need for an underlying subject is just as evident in these instances. So says neuroscientist Masud Husain in *Our Brains, Our Selves*, the book referenced earlier.

This has been emphasized too by Todd Feinberg, a neurologist and psychiatrist who has treated patients with Alzheimer's, epilepsy, traumatic brain injury (TBI), brain tumors and strokes. Feinberg concludes his book *Altered Egos: How the Brain Creates the Self* with a resounding affirmation of the self.

> "I believe the evidence supports the existence of a Kantian "I" at the center of each of us that is the subject of our conscious experience and the core of our being. The margins of the "I"

203 Stephen Braude, *First Person Plural: Multiple Personality and the Philosophy of Mind* (Rev. ed., Lanham, MD: Rowman & Littlefield, 1995), 173.

204 Stephen E. Braude, "Counting Persons and Living With Alters," PPP / Vol. 10, No. 2 /June 2003, 188, 156.

> are not entirely fixed, however, and they change throughout one's life. The patients in this book with altered egos demonstrate the dramatic, surprising, and sometimes frightening flexibility of the margins of the self. While the many parts of the brain create the self, however, there is no specific material locus of the self or the inner "I" within the brain."[205]

Mental disorders are the result of malfunctions of the brain caused by chemical imbalances or synaptic changes or injuries. But even in disorders ranging from amnesia to insanity, it can hardly be denied that the human person retains a first-person perspective. Even in these abnormal conditions, the self is known in every implicit or explicit first-person act whether in understanding and reasoning or in various conscious states or in a whole range of intentional activities. In our experience of remembering, we often struggle to remember some past event. In the present context the question we should ask is: who is doing the struggling?

In the face of such intellectual obstacles, physicalists like Dennett were reduced to declaring that "third-person absolutism" will simply serve as the foundation of their positions—an absolutism because it is based on dogma and not argument.

But this statement of belief cannot be taken seriously since the burden of proof remains on those who deny the self. Its existence is especially apparent at a biological level. As frequently noted, each one of the tens of thousands of molecules constituting each one of our neurons is in continuous transit, changing approximately 10,000 times in a normal life-span. In fact, it is not just our neurons but every cell in our body that is regularly replaced. But, despite the constant flux at the neuronal and other levels, something remains the same—or we could not even continue reading just this sentence!

205 *Altered Egos: How the Brain Creates the Self* (London: Oxford University Press, 2001), 149.

Self-Denying Philosophers

The most influential denier of the "I" was David Hume. In a famous passage in his *A Treatise of Human Nature*, Hume declared, "When I enter most intimately into what I call myself, I always stumble on some particular perception or other, of heat or cold, light or shade, love or hatred, pain or pleasure. I never can catch myself at any time without a perception, and never can observe any thing but the perception. … [Someone who believes in the self] may, perhaps, perceive something simple and continued, which he calls himself; though I am certain there is no such principle in me. I may venture to affirm of the rest of mankind, that they are nothing but a bundle or collection of different perceptions, which succeed each other with an inconceivable rapidity, and are in a perpetual flux and movement."

Here Hume, of course, assumes the existence of a self simply by assuming that he (meaning "I") can't find "myself." What is it that unifies his various experiences, that enables him to be aware of the external world and that remains the same throughout? Who is asking these questions? He assumes that "myself" is an observable state like his thoughts and feelings. But, as noted, the self is not something that can be thus observed. It is a constant fact of experience and, in fact, the ground of all experience.

And yet Hume's intellectual descendants ruled the roost until quite recently. Over the last century they shredded the self with an impressive variety of slicers and dicers. "Self"-denial was the order of the day.

Immanuel Kant had spoken of the self as an "imaginary focus" with no tangible reality (although he did believe in a unifying 'transcendental self').

Bertrand Russell said that "The word 'I' is grammatically convenient, but does not describe a datum."[206]

206 Bertrand Russell, *A History of Western Philosophy* (New York: Simon and Schuster, 1945), 567.

Some philosophers said that the "I" is simply a series of brain-states. Yet others pointed out that there is no continuing "I", just a series of "person-phases" or "I-thoughts."

The first group claimed that whatever we think of when we say "I" is simply constituted by the continuity of my physical body; a variant of this bodily continuity approach is the so-called animalist view.

The second group adopted a different approach and said that the "I" is simply the continuity of certain psychological features such as memories or desires.

Another group claimed that the "I" is simply a grammatical mistake.

The "bodily continuity" claim has a fatal flaw because any attempt to show that the "I" is purely the body ends up being circular. To show that the body is the "I", points out Madell, you have to not only assume the existence of an "I" but also that you can already identify and be aware of the "I." There is no way to verify an experience as mine without independently knowing the "I" and knowing the experience as mine. Our experience of the first-person shows that persons cannot be seen as being like any other objects in the physical world. Moreover, continues Madell, whereas physical objects exist in two dimensions, time and space, our experiences exist in three: time, space and subjectivity. The self-denier has no place either for the subject of experience or the first-person perspective.

Concerning the psychological continuity argument, the idea that "person" is simply a word used to describe various moments of consciousness is, on the face of it, absurd. There is an obvious continuity and unity to all our experiences. Just completing this sentence shows that we are not a series of selves performing individual acts of thought but one consciousness unifying a succession of acts. Madell has argued that our undeniable fear of future pain cannot be explained if the self is simply a collection of psychological elements. If we are told that we will undergo the most horrendous suffering in the distant future but that our psyche will be totally changed and we will lose our memory, we will not thereby be comforted. The awareness of a continuing identity is unshakable.

What about the idea that the "I" is simply a grammatical mistake? Gilbert Ryle, in his *The Concept of the Mind* dismissed what he called "the systematic elusiveness of the I" as a grammatical feature and said "I" is no different than "here" and "this" in being unanalyzable. None of these words actually refer to anything. But, as Madell and other thinkers have shown, "here" and "this" are defined in the context of an "I" and are in fact parasitic on "I." "Here" and "this" are understood relative to "I." It is only "I" that is unanalyzable while referring to something definite.

As we have seen, the most recent trend was the use of thought-experiments to resolve the issue but these turned out to be scientifically and conceptually flawed.

Self-Denying Scientists

Joseph LeDoux in *The Synaptic Self* said that "given the importance of synaptic transmission in brain function, it's practically a truism to say that the self is synaptic. What else could it be?"[207]

Although this sounds like a crudely physicalist attempt to pinpoint the neural location of the self, LeDoux explains that his goals are more modest.

He says in an interview,

> "To the extent that we are a product of our genes and experiences, we are our synapses. This doesn't mean that the essence of who you are is encoded at a particular synapse. It means that your self is

---

207 Joseph LeDoux, *The Synaptic Self: How Our Brains Become Who We Are* (New York: Viking, 2002), 2.

> a very complex pattern of synaptic connectivity in your brain."[208]

There can be no question that our genes and our interaction with our environment help form our personalities, beliefs and dispositions and, at least at certain levels, the "forming" is done by the wiring of the synapses. But this has no bearing on the entirely different question of the unitary intellectual self underlying who we are and how we act. In her review of Le Doux's book, Susan Blackmore, a convinced physicalist, rightly points out that "The "self" of the title is more like personality, or the sum of our brain's activities. … But his stirring conclusion that 'You are your synapses' is less than convincing."[209]

LeDoux does not exclude other ways of understanding the self. He notes that

> "many people will counter that the self is psychological, social or spiritual, rather than neural, in nature. My assertion that synapses are the basis of personality does not assume that your personality is *determined* by synapses; it's the other way around. Synapses are simply the brain's way of receiving, storing and retrieving our personalities, as determined by all the psychological, cultural and genetic factors. So as we begin to understand ourselves in neural, especially synaptic, terms, we do not have to sacrifice the other ways of understanding existence."[210]

In his typically piercing review of *The Synaptic Self*, Jerry Fodor writes: LeDoux says "the big question brain researchers should be asking: 'What makes us who we are?'" To this, Fodor says,

> "it is less than entirely clear exactly which question he thinks this is, or why he thinks that it is brain scientists who should be trying to answer it. Let's start by clearing this up a bit. Philosophers like

208 Claudia Dreifus, "A Conversation with Joseph LeDoux: Taking a Clinical Look at Human Emotions," *New York Times*, October 8, 2002.

209 Susan Blackmore, "Serotonin, ergo sum," *New Scientist*, March 2 2002, http://www.newscientist.com/article/mg17323325.900-serotonin-ergo-sum.html.

210 *The Synaptic Self*, op. cit.

> to worry about what they call 'the problem of personal identity', which deals with the question: 'What about me might change, consonant with my remaining who I am?'"

As framed, Fodor points out that this question

> "isn't one that it would be reasonable to expect brain science to answer. I mention it by way of contrast with what is worrying LeDoux."

Ledoux's thesis is "You are your synapses. They are who you are." Of this Fodor says

> "it is not exactly clear what it means. But, whatever exactly it does, I doubt that anything of the sort is true." It is problematic on two grounds. First there is the level of analysis: it is unlikely that psychological states and processes are implemented only at the cell and synapse level: "The very fact that different regions of the brain often serve different psychological functions strongly suggests that it should not."
>
> Moreover, "the sum and substance, so far, is that LeDoux (and, I fear, many of his neuropsychological colleagues) is working on a model for a brain that implements an associationist psychology. That is, no doubt, much the direction Hume would have predicted that cognitive neuroscience was likely to take. The objection to the program, however, is that it has become harder and harder to believe that the psychology of the cognitive mind is primarily associative. This is, of course, a very long story. … The main difference between our cognitive science and Hume's is that we know about computers and Hume didn't. That is why we don't have to be associationists, though he did."[211]

LeDoux was neutral on the self as traditionally understood. But two other recent scientific works aggressively sought to dissolve the self. The first was *The Mind is Flat: The Illusion of Mental Depth and the*

211 *Times Literary Supplement*, May 17 2002.

Improvised Mind by psychologist Nick Chater and the second *Being You: A New Science of Consciousness* by neuroscientist Anil Seth.

Chater affirms that "almost everything we know about our minds is a hoax, played on us by our brains" and "talk of being conscious of one's self is incoherent nonsense—'selves', after all, aren't part of the sensory world."

In his review of the book, Raymond Tallis highlights its obvious errors:

> "The Mind is Flat … illustrates how reducing persons or selves to their brains—what we may call 'brainifying' the person—invariably involves personifying the brain and treating it as if it were, after all, a kind of self. The brain, Chater tells us, perpetrates "hoaxes", "solves problems", "is continuously scrambling to link together scraps of sensory information", trying to organize and interpret them. All of this is, "in a very real sense mindless"—although (with a characteristic wobble) Chater asserts that we (italics mine) are "relentless improvisers, powered by a mental engine, perpetually creating meaning from sensory input." How very like a self!"
>
> We do not need psychologists to tell us that we won't find the self by examining the brain and that brains are fundamentally different from selves. For example, the state of the brain at given time is confined to what it is at that time. It cannot reach out to its own past, not even to those past events that have shaped it, or to its future, or to the timeless zone of general meanings and facts that we take account of to make sense of our lives. … Brains could fool us into believing that we are or have selves only, *per impossibile*, by borrowing the capacities that actual minds (persons, selves) have. That I am a self is hardly something I can be mistaken about. … Selfhood, Zahavi concludes, is inseparable from the quality that experience has of being first-personal, of being *mine*."[212]

212 https://philosophynow.org/issues/129/Brains_Minds_Selves

In *Being You*, Anil Seth claims that the experience of 'being you'—or 'being me'—is a collection of perceptual best guesses, of internally directed controlled hallucinations.

But who does the guessing or has the hallucination?

Occasionally, he slips in "the brain" as a substitute for "self" — "When the brain is figuring out what-in-the-world is part of its body" or "The brain generates and deploys predictive models."

Here the brain is acting as the central director and planner. The problem, as we have seen, is that the brain is nothing but a constantly fluctuating storm of electricity and chemistry. The brain does not do any "figuring out." A continuously identical self does that.

The self-contradiction in self-denial surfaces constantly. For instance, he writes, "The idea I've been proposing for many years now …" We ask: Who is this "I" that has been "proposing" the idea?

Tallis finds Seth's thesis of controlled hallucinations implausible.

> "If, moreover, the brain generates only a 'top-down fantasy', how would we get to know this supposed truth about our experience? By what means would we get past the fantasy to call it out? 'Science!' is not an answer here because ultimately science too depends on perceptions. If perception were the ever-deceptive epistemological prisoner of the brain, there would be no means by which scientists could expose what the brain is up to, never mind share the news that daily experience is a controlled hallucination.
>
> It would appear, after all, then, that the 'neuronal fantasy' is so completely reined in by reality that it is not a fantasy at all. Sense experience is no kind of *hallucination*, controlled or otherwise. If I have the experience of seeing a cup in front of me and there is a cup in front of me (as is usually the case), this is not a question of experiencing any kind of hallucination, controlled or not."[213]

213 https://philosophynow.org/issues/149/Perception_as_a_Controlled_Hallucination

Michael Pollan, who interviewed Seth, is likewise unimpressed by his central thesis:

> "Who is the subject of these mental operations? It is Seth's contention that there is no who. 'You don't need an inferrer to make inferences or a perceiver to make perceptions,' he told me … For me it doesn't quite add up. I don't doubt that all these operations may well be going on under the hood, the brain making its best guesses and presenting me with the hallucinated world and self, but doesn't there eventually have to be a subject, a me, who actually experiences these emotions and colors? And if this self is an illusion, then *whose* illusion is it? … The way I see it there is an unbridgeable gulf between the brain's operations as a prediction machine and my felt experience of the resulting hallucination. How can you have a hallucination without a hallucinator? …
>
> It appears we have found our way back to the hard problem—the problem of explaining how to connect the operations of the brain to the felt fact of first-person experience. To be fair to Seth, he doesn't claim to have solved the hard problem."[214]

Postmortem

Persistent critics might say that what we call the "I" is a product of a network of neurons and the network continues despite the changes in its constituents. Moreover, evolution shows different organisms that also retain their identities and *homo sapiens* is just the latest in a long line. What we call a sense of identity comes from a feedback loop. There is no mystery about the source of our continuing identity: It is DNA.

The outlandish claim about DNA being the source of the "I" is similar to the many DNA myths propagated by hucksters. Claims like DNA analysis reveals our IQ or athletic skills or the kinds of wine we would like. Scientists point out that this is all nonsense.

---

214 Michael Pollan, *A World Appears: A Journey into Consciousness* (New York: Penguin Press. 2026), 193.

According to the Human Genome Research Institute, DNA is "the molecule that carries genetic information for the development and functioning of an organism." It enables our "functioning" by making all the proteins in the body. It is entirely physical; it is made up of chemical building blocks (nucleotides). The chemical information specific to you is passed on to successive generations via DNA. In this respect, DNA maintains our individual physical continuity.

But there is nothing about DNA that is "conscious" or "self-like." Note too that genes are not conscious and do not think. They are incapable of awareness, let alone awareness of continued self-identity. Plainly, conscious self-identity cannot reside in something that is neither conscious nor cogitative, i.e., DNA.

The would-be slayer of the self then switches gears and claims that the apparent "I" is nothing but a network of neurons or a mass of molecules. In other words, you, the self-slayer, are asserting that "you" are nothing but fluctuating electrochemical hives of activities riding off in all directions all the time. No molecule remains the same, no electrical pulse is static, no neuro-transmitter stays still. But this claim also results in incoherence.

This is the reason why: Here you are, standing in front of me and making a series of apparently reasoned arguments that claim "you" are actually a flash mob of neural firings while apparently remaining the self-same individual even as you are making the arguments. But if "you" are actually a medley of molecules playing musical chairs, a multitude of demons creating "pandemonium" (as envisioned by Dennett, et al.), how can there be a "you" that is unified and stays the same long enough to even make these arguments? And how can you even formulate these arguments given that the ceaseless physical change in the brain cannot allow you to complete a sentence?

You reply that everything physical in your brain is changing constantly, but its neural structures remain the same and, therefore, it is still "you" in a physical sense. For good measure, you add that a feedback loop provides the impression of the "I."

Again, this response does nothing to help the case. If all the neurons in the brain's neural networks change all the time, this means the networks are themselves changing all the time. There is no network separate from the neurons that make it up just as there is no bloodstream separate from the red and white blood cells and the platelets and plasma that comprise it. The bloodstream keeps changing as its components change. In the case of the brain's neural structures, we are still left with the problem with which we started: "You" would be nothing but a cluster of particles. And this means there can be no continuing "you" and there cannot even be a completed argument.

In response, you say that the "I" is generated by the brain's feedback loop. But this, again, solves nothing. Feedback loops relate to the outputs from a system that affect the system itself by either moving it toward or away from equilibrium. But this mechanism of actions and reactions found all across Nature relates purely to the physical equilibrium state of a biological system.

If a feedback loop could create an "I," it would be creating "I"s all across cellular systems in Nature. Also, it has been observed that the very idea of a feedback loop creating an "I" requires the loops to achieve consciousness and then loop back on themselves. Yet, it is obvious that the ever-changing physical substrate cannot support consciousness let alone create it. Even in the impossible instance of a feedback loop creating an "I," we are still left with the original problem of how the "I" could remain the same in the midst of the endless neuronal change.

Another escape route is to claim that the brain is a self-organizing system, and this is the "I." But self-organizing systems are found across Nature, and none of them produce "I"s. And, of course, this is not the issue. Even if a self-organizing system pulls off the impossible and magically creates an "I," the "I" would be made up of neurons that never stay the same. And we are back where we began.

Not to be deterred, you say that even if we do not know how the brain creates the appearance of the "I," the brain itself is the product of evolution, and the "I" emerged because it provided an advantage in terms of survival. But this is just as much an evasion of the undeniable issue as all the others. The brain's evolutionary history is not the issue here. What we are pointing to is our undeniable experience today of being unified, enduring persons who think and act.

Our continuing self-identity is inexplicable if it is physical because the physical substrate does not retain its self-identity from moment to moment as we unmistakably do.

You switch gears, yet again, and say that the idea of a non-physical "I" is clearly mistaken because all mental activity, including the idea of the "I," comes from the brain. Therefore, it has to be physical although we do not understand how. Science will close this gap as it has closed other gaps in the past. But this last resort argument leads nowhere. It is science that led us to the definitive finding that the brain is made up of electrical and chemical processes that are in perpetual motion.

But here is a bigger problem: How is it possible to hold that matter can "produce" non-physical phenomena? Scientific laws apply only to physical quantities that can be physically measured. In this discussion, we are talking of a set of physical quantities (the brain) giving rise to something that is not a measurable quantity. But this means we are no longer making a scientific claim since science can only deal with quantities. And since we are leaving the purview of science, the question becomes: How do we know that such things happen—that the physical can give rise to the non-physical? Clearly, this is an affirmation that cannot be demonstrated. And what are the laws that govern the relationship between the physical and the non-physical? And how can we account for the relationship?

The discovery of the constant physical change in the brain has a radical and irreversible impact on how we can understand ourselves. The question is: How can something be relatively stable and enduring if it is intrinsically ever-changing? How can I be the same single person from moment to moment if "I" am nothing but a multitude of constantly changing molecules?

Neuroscience makes it clear that the brain is nothing but an assemblage of chemical messengers and electrical signals and goes further by showing that all the physical components of the brain are in constant change. It is a hard fact that there is nothing that stays the same in your brain in the same way that you retain your identity as an "I." Nor is there something in your brain that is able to perform operations constantly as the same continuing "I." We cannot be having this discussion if my "I" or your "I" was in constant flux or not unified and indivisible. You could not have an education and then use that education in performing certain tasks if there was no continuity between the entity that received the education and the entity that later performed the tasks derived from the education. Our immediate experience shows that the "I" is unified and continuous.

Insanity, Imbecility or Ignorance?

David Lund sums up the insuperable difficulties facing physicalism:

> "It cannot acknowledge the occurrent reality of our conscious states." And this means we have to reject "a belief whose truth one cannot consciously deny without also presupposing it to be true."
>
> It cannot "acknowledge that there is any important unity of consciousness (let alone the irreducible unity for which I argue in this book), for the appearance of unity can hardly prove to be anything more than a veneer, thinly masking its underlying material foundation—consisting of billions of individual nerve cells engaged in enormously complex physical activity. The picture of such a hoard of individual activities could hardly be further from one of an underlying singleness or unity. Yet the experience of a unified consciousness is undeniable."
>
> It "cannot recognize any genuine agency, as it cannot acknowledge that a person is a self-determining being capable of choosing among genuine alternative courses of action that make it true that she could have acted other than as she did. Yet it is freedom in this sense that we all presuppose in practice. In first-person terms, I find it impossible to deny that my conscious intentional actions originate with me, as opposed to being links in continuous causal chains extending indefinitely far into the past."

Consciousness is a fundamental reality that cannot be reduced to or seen as emerging from "any assembly of nonconscious physical things." And

> "We cannot view from a standpoint outside our subjective experience the relation between consciousness and the nonconscious physical reality out of which it is assumed to arise and to which it is claimed to be reducible. … No reductive effort, however, intensive

> or sophisticated, can be evaluated or understood apart from the essential involvement of the phenomenon it attempts to reduce."

This leads back to the self, the subject of consciousness.

> "To acknowledge the irreducible reality of consciousness with its intrinsic subjectivity should lead us, I have argued, to acknowledge that there is a conscious subject at its center, in that it exists in virtue of its constitutive involvement in the states of the conscious subject or self whose consciousness it is."[215]

As we have seen, experiences by their nature call for the existence of the self.

In the final analysis, the fundamental fallacy of physicalism lies in its failure to correspond with human experience. The very affirmation of physicalism is an affirmation of its being in utter error. We are told to believe there are no beliefs. We are asked to be conscious of the fact that we cannot be conscious. We are asked to affirm as truth that there is no truth, to understand that we cannot understand. Learned scholars assure us that they do not exist and deploy abstruse arguments to show that their own reasoning is nothing but a matter of electricity and chemistry.

Physicalism cannot work because it contradicts everything in our experience. Critics might say that this is a case of placing alleged common sense or folk psychology against verified science much like preferring alchemy to chemistry. This allegation is mistaken because it derives from the same superficial kind of slogan-think that gave rise to physicalism in the first place. We are not talking here of an empirical study of some physical domain, e.g., chemistry or astronomy. We are talking about what is required for performing any empirical study, the ability to experience another reality.

215 David Lund, *The Conscious Self*, op cit., 13, 14, 20, 385, 386.

Experience reigns supreme when we are talking of the very act of experiencing. All other judgments concern judgments made about an external reality, interpretations of perceived phenomena and the like. But with consciousness, thought and the self we are dealing with something we directly apprehend: there is no interpretive filter, no inferential process. We are talking of the fact of our experiencing not about facts "out there."

Folk chemistry may have been wrong on the elements and their molecular interaction. Folk cosmology may have been wrong on the origin and structure of planetary systems. Folk psychology, on the other hand, is a different matter: there is no such thing as "folk psychology." Rather, we are considering here our capacity to be conscious, to think and to intend as unitary beings: it is not something that we step back and dissect as in all the other areas of learning. It is, instead, our very ability to dissect, to integrate, to extrapolate.

These are the relevant considerations in any study of physicalist arguments. It is only in an asylum that we need arguments to support the testimony of our immediate experience. For "normal" people, what is self-evident requires no argument if it is stacked up against the merely speculative (especially if the latter is wildly implausible to begin with).

My ultimate proof is my own experience: to be taken seriously, argument and speculation must not only be plausible but be compatible with what I KNOW to be the case in my experience.

In the present context, the burden of proof is on the physicalist who wants to deny what is all-pervasive and undeniable. Why should I not trust what is obvious in my experience? More important, no argument can "disprove" what is self-evident. Such an argument demonstrates only one thing: that the arguer is not attentive to the ground of his/her personal experience. The burden of proof remains on those who do not want to accept the veracity of what is obvious and we have no obligation to consider their arguments if we want to go with what is obvious. You might say "science" has shown that many "obvious" beliefs like "the world is flat" were wrong. But we are not talking about particular empirical judgments here. We are talking about fundamental insights and our very capacity to make empirical judgments.

It would be helpful to clarify what is meant by "obvious." We are talking here about fundamental pre-scientific and pre-philosophical insights: that are assumed by science and logic: insights that I *see* to be the case. At best we can draw attention to such insights but we cannot prove or disprove them. This is why they are called self-evident.

There is no reason why I have to defend or give up any of these beliefs that are obvious in my immediate experience. These are not empirical or logical. They are part of our very infrastructure of thought: they not only make thinking possible but are presupposed by the very possibility of our experiencing anything.

At some point it has to be recognized that the physicalist position is not simply untenable but incompatible with sanity.

The consistent physicalist has to hold the following views:

> There is no "I" or "You"
>
> There are no such things as beliefs and desires. For that matter, there is no such thing as feeling pain.
>
> There is no such thing as "life" in the sense of autonomous agency. There are only collections of chemicals that inexorably follow specific sets of physical laws.
>
> There is no world of conscious experience. What we think of as "being conscious" is simply an illusion. All we have are interacting quantum fields.
>
> There is no freedom since we are simply physical particles that inexorably obey all the laws of matter. This also means

there is no such thing as "love" since this implies a free giving of oneself to another.

There are no actions of persons since there are no intentions. There are only movements of neurons and limbs and vocal cords.

There is no "meaning" or "understanding." To mean or to understand there has to be someone who can encode and decode meaning, who understands and communicates.

There are no concepts because this would mean (contrary to the physicalist premise) that you can go from particular things, from sensations, to ideas that transcend the specific and the concrete. In other words, there is no such thing as language.

There can be no conversation or dialogue because that would imply two people who can "mean" and "understand" and use concepts.

In talking to a skeptic, we have to press this point. Everything in our everyday experience testifies to our reality as conscious subjects capable of free rational thought and intention. But all the arguments raised by you the skeptic point in the opposite direction. For too long we have tolerated this contradiction. It is time to get serious and for you to answer these questions:

Are you conscious?

Do you speak and communicate which means do you use symbols to represent physical objects or concepts that do not refer to specific physical objects?

Do you use the first person perspective?

If you say that your conscious, intellective and volitional acts are strictly activities of neurons, then you are saying these are simply movements of matter. And matter, let it be said, ultimately comes down to quantum fields interacting at random. You cannot talk of quantum fields thinking in concepts and symbols or having a first person perspective. If you actually act on your beliefs, you would have to be housed in secure psychiatric facilities.

All skeptical claims are self-contradictory because they all assume that there is:

> No consciousness
>
> No thinking
>
> No self
>
> No purposes or reasons,
>
> Everything is reducible to random interactions of quantum fields.

But you cannot practice these beliefs no matter how fervently you hold them. If you try to defend them, you end up contradicting yourself because you have to assume that there is a unified subject who is capable of rational thought, making judgments and performing intentional acts—all of which you deny. Perception, thought and action are all activities of a unified subject.

For too long we have taken the skeptics seriously. It is time to call the bluff, to point out that the emperors are wearing no clothes and we can see through them. Let them practice what they profess first before we take them seriously. If they object, ask them: who is objecting?

From Musical Chairs to a Paradigm-Shift

We noted that there is a fascinating parallel to the dilemma for physicalism that emerged by the end of the twentieth century and continues to confront the scientific community today. It is the dilemma that confronted scientists at the end of the nineteenth century. By the end of that century, prominent scientists, most notably Lord Kelvin, had already begun speaking of the end of physics pointing out that its main features had been laid out and no major mysteries loomed ahead. As an aside, these scientists noted that only two puzzles remained to be solved: the Michelson-Morley experiment that failed to show the existence of the ether and the phenomenon of black-body radiation. Astoundingly, it was precisely these two problems that ended up giving birth to the theories of relativity and quantum mechanics, rewriting the roadmap of physics and changing our whole understanding of physical reality.

The scientific community faces a similar impasse today. Questions about the nature of conscious beings, intellective capabilities and the human self remain as intractable as ever. The optimistic forecasts that these mysteries would be rapidly eliminated, made as long ago as the nineteenth century, have dissolved into handwaving and long-defaulted physicalist promissory notes. Investigations into consciousness and language have shown that the current paradigm cannot hold.

Paradoxically, the dogmatic physicalism of the present day resembles nothing more clearly than the simple-minded thinking of pre-scientific times. Any inquiry that went beyond the plain observation that the sun rose in the east and set in the west was strenuously resisted because of the possibility that the resultant conclusions would threaten the dogmas of the day. Likewise, today, inquiries into the nature of consciousness, thought and the self that go beyond the firing of neurons are feared and prohibited.

Subtlety, complexity, quests into "there be dragons" territory are impermissible because they are simply too threatening to certain contemporary pieties.

The change from Ptolemy to Copernicus or Newton to Einstein did not come without blood, sweat and tears. The contemporary situation is no different. Desperate attempts are made to shore up traditional positions in the face of new and often conflicting data. Polemical attacks are now considered acceptable substitutes for serious discussion.

But gradual positive changes in both scientific and philosophical domains (recognition of the "hard problem" in science and a movement away from unblinking materialism and reductionism in philosophy) may be heralds of an eventual paradigm shift.

Which brings us to the new framework of thought created by AI.

IV

"THERE'S MAGIC IN THE WEB OF IT"

THE PLOYS of the physicalists who reject the hard facts of experience help us understand the allure of AI as a stand-in for humankind. Paradoxically, the physicalists' distorted depiction of humans is actually an accurate description of AI systems.

The main physicalist theories of mind have a physical nexus for all activities. They do not see any semantics in the world. It's all syntax. Since physicalists "think" that thinking is entirely a neurological process that is physical through and through, it's senseless to talk of truth or meaning.

Now, while none of this is true when it comes to humans, they do apply to AIs. AIs indeed are Dennett's "syntactic engines" and not semantic processors like us. AIs don't have beliefs or desires which is what Paul Churchland "believes" to be the case with humans. The idea that AIs have a self is an illusion as our physicalist self-deniers say about themselves.

If we could re-direct physicalists' passionate proclamations of the absence of consciousness, thought and self from humans to AIs, we would kill two birds with one stone. We would break two spells with one move. All that wasted time and effort in denying the undeniable could now be usefully re-deployed in affirming the obvious.

There are two other paradoxes that lie in wait for the physicalists.

Contrary to the common idea that AIs think like humans, any study of their "inner lives" will show that their operations are entirely mathematical. No emotions, feelings, strokes of genius, intellectual inspiration—only algebra, geometry, calculus, statistics, probability theory.

With linear algebra and geometry, words and images are translated into mathematical formats so as to identify relationships, find patterns and situate context. Words become lists of numbers (vectors). Images become rows and columns of numbers (matrices). These are plotted in a space of many dimensions where birds of a feather can flock together, i.e., similar data points cluster together.

On the "outside," the AIs provide simulations that could mislead us into believing that they operate in a human-like fashion.

The crowning paradox here is the fact is that many of the greatest mathematicians were Platonists and not physicalists and the triumph of AI, a mathematical creation, is by extension a triumph of the non-physical human intellect. The history of AI is closely correlated with the history of mathematics —and mathematicians!

When the smoke of confusion clears, we find that AI is proof that physicalism is false!

Before going further, we need to know how today's AIs landed in the middle of muddles about the mind. The ideas that AIs "understand" or are conscious arise from a concatenation of confusions. Let's start with these.

A Concatenation of Confusions

The physicalists said that AIs "understand" in the human way but humans themselves cannot "understand" —as Dennett phrased it, we have "competence without comprehension."

Many AIers believe artificial neural networks behave the same way as the human brain and so they reflect the way we think. Neuroscientists disagree emphatically with the idea that these networks mirror the brain. Francis Crick, who worked in neuroscience and with neural networks "chafed at what he saw as fundamental biological inadequacies in these programs, in particular their lack of anatomical and physiological accuracy. One thing that particularly especially annoyed him was their reliance on backprop [backpropagation—a key concept in artificial neural networks]—'it seems highly unlikely that this actually happens in the brain,' he wrote."[216]

The AI engineers largely ignored the concerns raised by Crick and other neuroscientists: "Most simply got on with their work, producing increasingly impressive pieces of software and quite understandably showing no interest in linking their work to the anatomy or physiology of the brain."[217]

Just as the physicalists were led astray by speculative metaphors, analogies and thought-experiments, many AIers are misled by the terms they use—terms that blur the distinction between machines and mortals.

There is no similarity between lightning and a lightning bug.

---

216 Matthew Cobb, *The Idea of the Brain: The Past and Future of Neuroscience*, op cit., 277.

217 Ibid., 278

Likewise, random access memory in a computer is in no way like human memory which involves storage and retrieval processes in the brain as well as concepts and subjectivity. With regard to the biology of memory, Cobb writes, "We are still far from understanding what is happening when we remember. Our brains might be like a computer in terms of how they sometimes process information, but the way we store and recall our memories is completely different. We are not machines—or, rather, we are not like any machine we have yet built or can currently envisage."[218]

Machine "learning," which is simply mathematical processing, has no similarity to human learning, which is conceptual processing.

A programming language is a set of instruction-sets for computers and nothing like human languages which involve communication through concepts and the infinite use of finite means (i.e., a limited number of words being used in an unlimited number of sentences).

Computers are a collection of mechanisms whereas a human being is a unitary subject that unifies the various mechanisms found in the body.

Synthetic text generation, as found in generative AI, is qualitatively distinct from human thought and conversation.

Performing simulations of human interaction does not suggest the existence of a human-like intellect. As Shannon Vallor reminded us, an AI "is not a mind. It is a mathematical tool for extracting statistical patterns from past human-generated data."[219]

The genesis of these and other "confusions" lies in the overlapping worlds of software, neuroscience, psychology and philosophy of mind. So, we should think of the history and nature of AI in this light. Most

218 Ibid., 232.

219 Shannon Vallor, *The AI Mirror* (New York: Oxford University Press, 2024), 38.

important, we need to understand the precise purview of AI so as not to be misled by extravagant and irrelevant claims.

It's All Mathematics and Simulation

> "Mathematics is a system of symbols and accepted axioms created by human beings, which can be used as a language for describing the world. Math progresses when we pose the right problems and come up with comprehensible proofs. The qualities that led the 19th-century mathematician Carl Friedrich Gauss (1777-1855) to call mathematics the "queen of sciences"—its rigor, logic and isolation from real-world phenomena—are precisely what make it the realm of human inquiry that AI can best learn, imitate and expand on. But would autonomous AI mathematics be mathematics at all? As the mathematician and philosopher Reuben Hersh (1927-2020) argued, mathematics isn't only a human activity but a social phenomenon. All sorts of mathematical truths aren't properly part of what we refer to as mathematics unless they are discovered and explained by human beings. Progress in mathematics is a matter of communication; a proof that is poorly explained is no better than a proof that is wrong."
>
> —*Daniel Kipnis, "AI Can Do Math, but Is It Really Math?"*[220]

No one denies that AIs operate in a digitized artificial world created by us to perform functions on our behalf using mathematical symbols. We live in the real world of events, experiences, and people and we think and act on the basis of our conceptual and perceptual processing.

AIs "work" because of their mathematical mechanisms of action:

> Representing data (text, images, sounds) in the form of numbers (vectors, matrices, etc.) that become coordinates in a mathematical space

220 *https://www.wsj.com/opinion/ai-can-do-math-but-is-it-really-math-a7db34be*

> Recognizing patterns by calculating statistical relationships in terms of distances between the coordinates
>
> Applying statistical probability using patterns learned in training so as to generate responses to queries
>
> Using calculus to "learn" and optimize by quantifying errors and calibrating parameters

Chatbots respond to users by "translating" text into numbers and then applying linear algebra and probability.

Detailed descriptions of the complex mathematics involved in these processes will be Greek to the average layperson. But we can grasp the general principles involved just as we can understand the general processes involved in nuclear fission without knowing all of the physics behind them.

AIs are works of magic, the magic of mathematics.

Shannon Vallor delves into the details:

> "The surface of an AI mirror is the machine learning and optimization algorithm that determines which features of the 'incident light'—that is, the data the model is trained on—will be focused and transmitted back to us in the form of the model's outputs. It is the algorithm embedded in a machine learning model that expresses the *objective function* (a mathematical description of what an 'optimal solution' to the problem will look like). The learning algorithm and model hyperparameters determine how the training data are processed into a result as the model 'learns.' The algorithmic surface of the model determines which of the innumerable possible patterns that can be found within the data (the model's 'light') will be selected during model training as salient and then amplified as the relevant 'signal' to guide the model's outputs (the particular image of the data it reflects).

> These outputs, while more varied in type than the outputs of a glass mirror, are still constrained to specific data modalities and formats. Primarily what machine models are used to return are various kinds of predictions or classifications: numerical values, a binary yes vs. no, a risk source, a probability, a text label or a unique identifier, the likely next word in a sentence, or next move in a game or ranked list. … Generative AI models such as large language models predict lengthy strings of text, complex images, sounds, and videos, or extended series of commands."[221]

While it's all math, AI, at another level, is all simulation. AIs simulate human understanding, reasoning, speaking, acting and feeling. Inevitably, the danger is of mistaking the simulation for the reality being simulated.

A key step in moving beyond today's confusion is to understand the overlap among the histories of mathematics, neuroscience, philosophy of mind, computers and AI.

221 *The AI Mirror* (New York: Oxford University Press, 2024), 49.

Once Upon Three Centuries Ago

> "These three frameworks—rules and symbols, neural networks, and Bayesian models—offer complementary perspectives on the mind. Each framework highlights a different kind of mathematics that is ultimately going to be critical to understanding the Laws of Thought."[222]
>
> —*Tom Griffiths, The Laws of Thought: The Quest for a Mathematical Theory of the Mind*

As cognitive scientist Tom Griffiths tells the story, the magic of AI began at least in the 17th century. This is when Gottfried Wilhelm Leibniz began the centuries-long quest to use mathematics to discover the laws of human thought. The efforts of Leibniz, Descartes, George Boole and others culminated in the 20th century Cognitive Revolution that helped generate the AIs of today.

The thought-creations of these explorers of the mind converged with many of the technological breakthroughs of the last few decades: the Internet, data handling systems, cloud computing, versatile programming languages, algorithms, natural language processing, powerful processing chips, neural networks, Large Language Models, chatbots and much else. Today's neural networks and other AI platforms are the remarkable result of the ingenuity and painstaking efforts of thousands of visionary thinkers and tenacious engineers.

Consider these major milestones in the modern history of AI:

Date	**Milestone**
1936	The universal Turing machine—Alan Turing's blueprint for the modern computer
1943	Mathematical model of an artificial "neuron"—Warren McCulloch and Walter Pitts

222 op cit., xviii.

Date	**Milestone**
1950	The Turing Test, a framework to determine if a machine is "intelligent"—Alan Turing
1951	SNARC (Stochastic Neural Analog Reinforcement Calculator), the first artificial learning machine and the first simulated artificial neural network—Marvin Minsky
1956	First conference on AI held at Dartmouth College. The phrase "Artificial Intelligence" first used by John McCarthy.
1957	Perceptron, the first trainable algorithm—Frank Rosenblatt
1966	First chatbot (Eliza)—Joseph Weizenbaum
Seventies	Introduction of AI programming languages
Eighties	Expert Systems capturing knowledge specific to different domains. Failed to match expectations.
1986	Backpropagation algorithm and multi-layer neural networks—Geoffrey Hinton, David Rumelhart, Ronald Williams
1997	IBM's Deep Blue defeats world chess champion
2006	Deep learning—Geoffrey Hinton, Yoshua Bengio, and Yann LeCun
2011	IBM Watson wins Jeopardy
2017	Transformer neural networks
2022	Generative AI chatbot

Symbolic and Connectionist Computing

Until quite recently, AI was considered an esoteric novelty but not one that was relevant to everyday life. Even systems that beat boardgame champions and made scientific breakthroughs did not capture the public imagination.

All this changed with the coming of the LLMs and their associated chatbots.

Yes, these were trained by humans.

But they stood out because they could interact with human users instantly and credibly in a conversational mode.

As Griffiths emphasizes, the three cognitive science breakthroughs that led to today's AIs are "rules and symbols, neural networks, and probability theory."[223]

These breakthroughs were reflected in the two main approaches to AI computing, the first symbolic and the second connectionist. They reflect the two major forms of reasoning, deductive and inductive, with inductive being broken down into statistical and probabilistic inference.

In deductive reasoning, found in logic, we apply general principles to analyze the data under study. In inductive reasoning, found in science, we analyze the data under study to reach general principles or conclusions using statistical and probabilistic methods. With the first you start with rules and apply them to the data. With the second you start with the data to reach rules.

Symbolic AI uses symbols to represent information and applies pre-programmed rules and logic (if-then rules, inference engines, decision-trees, etc.) to solve problems and perform operations. All the processing was initially done on individual devices.

Connectionist AI does not start with inflexible rules but "learns" from "experience" using statistical and probability tools (for instance, assigning weights) applied to large quantities of data. The processing of the information is done in parallel on many processors spread across a network.

The most prominent current connectionist AI models are the systems called neural networks.

These simulate the human brain. They are loosely modeled on what was known decades ago of the ways in which actual neurons transfer and process information. Although analogous to the function and structure of biological neurons, there is no one-to-one mapping

223 Tom Griffiths, op cit., 294.

between artificial neural networks and the brain. Neither do neural networks have any bearing on such fundamental properties of the human intellect as subjectivity and abstraction.

The information processing nodes in the network, arranged in layers, represent neurons. The layers are arranged in a hierarchy comprising input and output nodes and multiple hidden layers where the input data are analyzed and then sent to the output node.

The information transfer connections between the nodes represent synapses. Just as synapses are weak or strong, the strength of these connections depend on their "weight."

The input nodes receive signals that are mathematically modeled to determine patterns and finally transmitted to output nodes.

The neural network "learns" from data through the algorithms used to "train" it. These algorithms automatically "recognize" patterns, connections and regularities in data of various kinds, be they textual, visual or something else.

The most notable of the neural networks are the transformer neural networks that set off the generative AI revolution. The "transformer" model is a neural network architecture used in natural language processing whereby text is broken down into certain tokens expressed in symbols that are then processed and analyzed. What is innovative about transformers is their ability (using a mathematical feature called self-attention) to analyze sequences of text or images or sounds, for instance sentences as opposed to just words, so as to determine patterns, relationships and context and enabling human-like responses.

Transformers form the backbone of the Large Language Models (LLMs) and the AI agents/chatbots that use these LLMs. Much of their power comes from their parallel processing hardware, the potency of their chips, the amount of data inputted into them (all public domain information on the internet, for instance), and the ingenious ways in which the system is trained.

Anything You Can Do, AI Can Do Better

The power of AI comes from its mathematical foundations as we see below.

Anil Ananthaswamy outlines the processes going on behind the scenes:

> We interact with an LLM in natural language—also called a prompt—and it produces some text. The output can at times seem a very well-reasoned response to the prompt, especially if the prompt involves a math/logic question. How does an LLM do that?...
>
> An LLM such as ChatGPT is trained on an enormous corpus of text, some of it in different languages, and some containing math, scientific content, and programming code. The training algorithm takes a sentence from the corpus of data, masks the last word, and asks the LLM to assign probabilities to all the words that it's trained on (its vocabulary); the LLM then chooses the word with the highest probability. ... At first, the LLM whose internal parameters have been randomly initialized, might predict the highest probability for some erroneous word. The training algorithm calculates an error, or loss, which can be understood as the difference between two probability distributions: one estimated by the model, which assigns probabilities to all the words in its vocabulary, and another where the correct word has a probability of 1 and the other words have zero probability. The loss is formulated as a function of the LLM's parameters; the algorithm uses backpropagation and some form of gradient descent to climb down the high-dimensional surface representing the loss and updates the parameters....
>
> Now, given the same sentence, the LLM will likely assign a higher probability to the correct word than before, resulting in a smaller loss. The algorithm repeats this process until the LLM correctly predicts the last word—not just for one sentence, but for nearly every sentence in the entire corpus.

> At this point, the LLM's parameters, or the weights of the connections between artificial neurons of the deep neural network, are statistically modeling not just the syntax of the written language, but even some of the semantics. This is self-supervised learning."[224]

Tom Griffiths spotlights the importance of probabilistic models in neural networks:

> "We can start to make sense of some of the abilities of large language models by thinking about them in probabilistic terms. Even though these models are based on neural networks, training them to predict the next word in a sequence means that they treat language as a probability distribution.
>
> We can also think of the way in which neural networks learn in terms of Bayesian inference: A configuration of weights is a hypothesis, and neural networks have an implicit prior distribution that favors hypotheses that are close to their initial weights. Each step of backpropagation moves them away from that initialization, but with limited data or limited amounts of training they will be biased towards their initial conditions. Exploring different neural network architectures—such as long short-term memory networks, or transformers—lets us find models with different expressive capacities and different inductive biases. …
>
> Having this probabilistic perspective on large language models is particularly important as they become an increasingly large part of AI systems that we interact with in our everyday lives, as it reveals some of their limitations. … As these systems are used to solve a wider range of problems, it is worth remembering that at their core they are systems to predict language, and sometimes doing a good job of predicting language is not the same thing as doing a good job of being an artificial general intelligence."[225]

---

224 *Why Machines Learn: The Elegant Math Behind Modern AI*, op cit., 433-4.

225 Tom Griffiths, *The Laws of Thought: The Quest for a Mathematical Theory of the Mind*, op cit., 292.

Tharin Pillay outlines the ways in which numbers are used to represent words and concepts and their relationships:

> "The key thing to see is that numbers encode space. We have an intuitive grasp of dimensions: we understand the difference between a line, a 2D video game, and a physical object. But mathematically, dimensions are just coordinates—a point in three-dimensional space can be represented with numbers (x, y, z)—and there's no limit to how many can exist. AI works by exploiting this fact: using thousands of numbers, a system learns to represent words and concepts as points in higher-dimensional latent space. For an entity like Claude, the concept "cat" is a comically long numerical string.
>
> AI systems are initially trained to predict the next token (a small chunk of information)—a simple task. But doing it well requires compressing information, which leads them to create intricate maps in latent space that encode not just words, but the relationships between them. Similar concepts are literally closer together: a string representing "cat" will be much closer to one representing "kitten" than to an unrelated one like "tax."
>
> This is radically different from traditional software, where fundamental concepts and rules are coded in by humans. There is no mystery in how Excel executes a formula; it's pre-programmed. But when AI generates a response, it makes use of intricate geometry we're just now learning to see."[226]

With these and other kinds of methodologies and innovations, AIs are able to perform tasks that were unimaginable in the past: dynamic "reasoning" and inference; personalized interactions; autonomous action; analysis of user emotions and sentiments with corresponding empathetic responses; and the generation of new content.

226 https://time.com/article/2026/06/15/ai-minds-consciousness-emotion/

There's AI and There's AI

Of course, generative AI is not the only AI game in town.

Notable progress has been made in biology through the application of "deep learning" as found in platforms like AlphaFold that predict the 3D structures of biomolecules. AI is likewise deployed in drug development, medical research, agriculture and most areas of human endeavor.

Another area of AI that continues to progress is the sphere of "intelligent" agents. Multi-agent systems existed long before generative AI. Autonomous AI agents, working in a common environment, collaborate to solve complex tasks or make decisions. New ground was broken here with the launch of a social network just for agents.

Yet another non-LLM approach to AI is taken by David Silver, a co-founder of Deep Mind, who seeks to create super-intelligent AI by building agents who learn from experience—but within simulations.

Also different (albeit at an early stage of development) are the so called "neuromorphic" companies that seek to match the "computational capacity" and "learning efficiency" of the human brain.

Robotics, although it has proven to be much more challenging, continues to progress.

With new breakthroughs announced on a regular basis, there is little doubt that the entire AI landscape will change constantly.

The "Turing Trap"

We have already seen why AI information-processing is as different from human thought as planes are from birds (to use Griffiths' analogy). We learn the principles of aerodynamics from birds and apply them in creating jets. But no sane person would mistake a jet for a bird.

When a user asks an LLM chatbot a question, the prompt is converted into tokens (symbols, words, parts of words) that are then given specific numerical values. Algebra, calculus, statistics, probability theory are then applied to generate a response. Algorithms (created by humans) detect patterns (in numerical terms) in digitized representations of huge datasets.

The LLM does not "understand" the meaning of words and sentences as humans do. There is no meaning-processing, no abstracting of concepts from percepts, no unitary subject who does the understanding and the intending. At the beginning and end of an LLM's operations, there are only numbers.

As David Bentley Hart clarifies,

> "In the physical functions of a computer, there is nothing resembling thought—no intentionality or anything remotely similar to intentionality, no consciousness, no unified field of perception, no reflective subjectivity. Even the syntax that generates coding has no actual existence *within* a computer. To think it does is rather like mistaking the ink, paper, glue, and typeface in a bound volume for the contents of its text. Meaning exists in the minds of those who write or use the computer's programs, but never within the computer itself."[227]

227 https://www.abc.net.au/religion/david-bentley-hart-narcissus-reflections-on-ai/102812590

The Achievement of AI

THE ACCOMPLISHMENTS OF AI to date are, of course, spectacular. Its potential is profound.

Flaws in data aggregation and analysis, biases, exclusions, exaggerations and the like were inevitable and will always plague AI. Abuses and destructive applications too are inescapable. These kinds of problems face all foundational technologies and call for continuous vigilance and improvement.

Dario Amodei, the founder of Anthropic, foresees the advent of the next generation of AI, what he calls "powerful AI," in the very near future.

> "By "powerful AI," I have in mind an AI model—likely similar to today's LLMs in form, though it might be based on a different architecture, might involve several interacting models, and might be trained differently—with the following properties:
>
> In terms of pure intelligence, it is smarter than a Nobel Prize winner across most relevant fields: biology, programming, math, engineering, writing, etc. This means it can prove unsolved mathematical theorems, write extremely good novels, write difficult codebases from scratch, etc.
>
> In addition to just being a "smart thing you talk to," it has all the interfaces available to a human working virtually, including text, audio, video, mouse and keyboard control, and internet access. It can engage in any actions, communications, or remote operations enabled by this interface, including taking actions on the internet, taking or giving directions to humans, ordering materials, directing experiments, watching videos, making videos, and so on. It does all of these tasks with, again, a skill exceeding that of the most capable humans in the world.

> It does not just passively answer questions; instead, it can be given tasks that take hours, days, or weeks to complete, and then goes off and does those tasks autonomously, in the way a smart employee would, asking for clarification as necessary.
>
> It does not have a physical embodiment (other than living on a computer screen), but it can control existing physical tools, robots, or laboratory equipment through a computer; in theory, it could even design robots or equipment for itself to use.
>
> The resources used to train the model can be repurposed to run millions of instances of it (this matches projected cluster sizes by ~2027), and the model can absorb information and generate actions at roughly 10–100x human speed. It may, however, be limited by the response time of the physical world or of software it interacts with.
>
> Each of these million copies can act independently on unrelated tasks, or, if needed can all work together in the same way humans would collaborate, perhaps with different subpopulations fine-tuned to be especially good at particular tasks.
>
> We could summarize this as a "country of geniuses in a datacenter."""[228]

Additionally, Anthropic has flagged the danger of AIs eventually being able to build their own successors with no human oversight:

> "We are delegating a growing share of AI development to AI systems themselves, which is speeding up our work. Taken far enough, and given enough compute, that trend points to an AI system capable of fully autonomously designing and developing its own successor. This is called *recursive self-improvement*. We are not there yet, and recursive self-improvement is not inevitable. But it could come sooner than most institutions are prepared for."[229]

228 https://www.darioamodei.com/essay/the-adolescence-of-technology

229 https://www.anthropic.com/institute/recursive-self-improvement

It is quite possible that Amodei's and Anthopic's predictions could come to pass. But even if they were realized, it will still remain a hard fact that AIs are not and will never be capable of human consciousness and thought.

"Powerful AI", as described by Amodei, or "recursive self-improvement" would still essentially be a work of mathematics just as nuclear fission will always remain a matter of sub-atomic behavior.

Trillions of mindless galaxies are intrinsically and irreducibly different from a single immaterial intellectual self.

Throwing all the data in the world at an LLM will not make it sentient.

Training an AI with every algorithm produced by the most intelligent living humans will not enable it to cross over from mathematics and simulation to subjective self-conscious meaning-processing.

This does not mean that AIs cannot become more powerful than their creators or wreak destruction on a global scale.

Amodei and Anthropic, in fact, accurately warn that these dangers are very real.

And Hart admits that

> "Conceivably, Artificial Intelligence could come to operate in so apparently purposive and ingenious a manner that it might as well be a calculating and thinking agency, but one of inconceivably enormous cognitive powers. A sufficiently versatile and capacious algorithm could very well endow it with a kind of "liberty" of operation that would mimic human intentionality, even though there would be no consciousness there—and hence no *conscience*—to which we could appeal if it "decided" to do us harm. The danger is not that the functions of our machines might become more like us, but rather that we might be progressively reduced to

> functions in a machine we can no longer control."[230]

But any major discovery and technology can be abused. The more powerful the technology, the greater the danger—think of nuclear energy or biological agents.

Despite these risks, the creation of AI—like the splitting of the atom—is a testament to the triumph of the human intellect. The triumph was effectuated by explorers deploying mathematics in the most innovative imaginable ways.

In his famous paper *The Unreasonable Effectiveness of Mathematics in the Natural Sciences*, Nobel Prize winner Eugene Wigner, another participant in our 1986 conference on AI, said

> "The statement that the laws of nature are written in the language of mathematics was properly made three hundred years ago. It is now more true than ever before. In order to show the importance which mathematical concepts possess in the formulation of the laws of physics, let us recall, as an example, the axioms of quantum mechanics. (...)
>
> It is difficult to avoid the impression that a miracle confronts us here, quite comparable in its striking nature to the miracle that the human mind can string a thousand arguments together without getting itself into contradictions, or to the two miracles of the existence of laws of nature and of the human mind's capacity to divine them."[231]

Given the fundamental role of mathematics in AI, it should be noted that many of the great mathematicians in history were Platonists.

Mathematical Platonists reject physicalism and hold that mathematics is a reality that exists independently of matter and human minds.

230 https://www.abc.net.au/religion/david-bentley-hart-narcissus-reflections-on-ai/102812590

231 https://www.maths.ed.ac.uk/~v1ranick/papers/wigner.pdf

The Platonists included three of the greatest mathematicians of all time:

> Georg Cantor—creator of set theory and the idea of infinity
>
> Gottlob Frege—founding father of modern logic and the philosophy of mathematics
>
> Kurt Gödel—The great logician colleague of Einstein who is especially known for Gödel's theorem

Other prominent Platonists included G.H. Hardy, Alonzo Church, Roger Penrose and Ian Hacking.

The takeaway for us is that AI is indisputably a mathematical creation. And mathematics in itself, according to many of its greatest practitioners, demonstrates the falsity of physicalism.

V

"CANST THOU NOT MINISTER TO A MIND DISEASED?"

MACBETH, ACT 5, SCENE 3

THE HUMAN RACE IS undergoing an identity crisis. Who are we and what are we?

This crisis was already in process long before AI arrived.

Descartes, Hume and Kant had already robbed us of our humanity. Descartes took away the body, Hume the intellectual self and Kant our confidence in our rationality.

A parade of physicalists then subjected us to one indignity after another.

AI dealt the final blow. Not only were we mere machines but our machines were more human than us!

Paradoxically AI itself, with its breathtaking reach and overwhelming impact, can rescue us from our "self"-doubt.

As we saw, AI represents the triumph of mathematics and of human ingenuity.

It spurs us on to re-discover the wonder of being human.

In fact, it can break the two spells with which we began.

If we think of the great miracles of the modern era—automotives, planes, phones, computers, life-saving drugs and healthcare interventions, agricultural plenty, energy generation and, now, AI—we realize that it is the human intellect, the human self, that is the driver of all these breakthroughs.

At least in terms of knowledge acquisition and material progress, the human experiment has been an outstanding success.

To be sure, all these efforts are constantly bedeviled by our own malicious and suicidal actions.

But, just as true, we see the power of the intellectual self manifested in its manifold creations.

For too long have we been anesthetized by the curated narratives of the physicalists. They dismissed the most obvious realities in our experience as illusions. They projected our own creations as powerful entities in their own right before which we were supplicants. None more so than AI.

But no more. We have woken up from the slumber of the spells and see ourselves for who we are.

Rediscovering the Wonder of Being Human

We humans are born into a mystery. What we encounter is a world of matter, trees, flowers, birds, insects, squirrels, tigers, and, at the center of it all, selfs: self-conscious, meaning-processing beings with a first person perspective.

We have no idea how any of these, let alone the last, the self, exists. How did reality come to be and come to be the way it is? How did we gain the capability of looking back at cosmic history? At the center of all our inquiry is the self that inquires. There is no explanation at all of the existence of a continuing self with all these powers of assembling data, inferring, speculating.

Neither the Big Bang nor the Cambrian Explosion can explain the "I" and the "you" or the first-person perspective. Quantum fields do not generate selfs. They just constitute our physical being.

In one final paradox, we find that the founders of modern science recognized the wonder of being human and, in fact, the wonder that is the world.

Let them have the last word.

Rediscovering Mind

"All matter originates and exists only by virtue of a force which brings the particle of an atom to vibration and holds this most minute solar system of the atom together. We must assume behind this force the existence of a conscious and intelligent *mind*. This *mind* is the matrix of all matter."[232]

—*Max Planck, the father of quantum physics*

"A conviction … of the rationality or intelligibility of the world lies behind all scientific work of a higher order … a belief bound up with deep feeling, in a superior *mind* that reveals itself in the world of experience."[233]

—*Albert Einstein, the discoverer of special and general relativity*

"I must premise, that I have nothing to do with the origin of the primary mental powers."

"I feel compelled to look to a First Cause having an intelligent *mind* in some degree analogous to that of man."[234]

—*Charles Darwin, the father of modern evolutionary theory*

"As followers of natural science we know nothing of any relation between thoughts and the brain, except as a gross correlation in time and space. (…) Biology cannot go far in its subject without being met by *mind*."[235]

—*Charles Scott Sherrington, pioneering Nobel Prize winning neurologist who discovered the synapse.*

"*Mind*, rather than emerging as a late outgrowth in the evolution of life, has existed always as the matrix, the source and condition of physical

232 Max Planck, *Das Wesen der Materie* [The Nature of Matter], speech at Florence, Italy (1944) (from Archiv zur Geschichte der Max-Planck-Gesellschaft, Abt. Va, Rep. 11 Planck, Nr. 1797).

233 Albert Einstein, *Ideas and Opinions*, trans. Sonja Bargmann (New York: Dell Publishing Company, 1973), 255.

234 Charles Darwin, *Origin of Species*, Chapter 7 on Instinct, https://brocku.ca/MeadProject/Darwin/1859_7.htmL; Charles Darwin, *The Autobiography of Charles Darwin*, https://www.update.uu.se/~fbendz/library/cd_relig.htm.

235 Charles Sherrington, *Man on his Nature* (New York: The Macmillan Company, 1941), 290-291.

reality (...) It is *mind* that has composed a physical universe that breeds life."[236]

—*Nobel Prize winning biologist George Wald*

"[Is mind] primary or an accidental consequence of something else? ... *Mind* was a primary part of nature from the beginning and we are simply manifestations of it at the present stage of history. It's not so much that *mind* has a life of its own but that *mind* is inherent in the way the universe is built."[237]

—*Freeman Dyson, Physicist, Institute for Advanced Studies*

236 George Wald, 1986 address to the First World Congress for the *Synthesis of Science and Religion*.

237 Interview with Freeman Dyson, *U.S. News and World Report*, April 18, 1988, 72.

About the Author

R.A. Varghese is the author and/or editor of various books on the mind-body problem and on science, philosophy, and religion. His *Cosmos, Bios, Theos*, included contributions from 24 Nobel Prize-winning scientists. *Time* magazine called *Cosmos* "the year's most intriguing book about God." *Cosmic Beginnings and Human Ends*, a subsequent work, won a Templeton Book Prize for "*Outstanding Books in Science and Natural Theology*." *The Wonder of the World* was endorsed by leading thinkers include two Nobel Laureates and was the subject of an Associated Press story. He co-authored *There is a God—How the World's Most Notorious Atheist Changed His Mind* with Antony. His work *The Missing Link* includes contributions from three Nobel Prize winners and scientists from Oxford, Cambridge, Harvard, and Yale. Varghese organized a conference on Artificial Intelligence and the Human Mind in 1986 at Yale University. Participants included four Nobel Prize winners and AI leaders from MIT, Stanford and Carnegie-Mellon. He was a panelist at the science and religion forum in the Parliament of World Religions held in Chicago in 1993 and an invitee and participant in the Millennium World Peace Summit of Religious and Spiritual Leaders held at the United Nations in August 2000.

www.ingramcontent.com/pod-product-compliance
Lightning Source LLC
LaVergne TN
LVHW050911210926
848482LV00012B/405
* 9 7 9 8 2 4 0 9 5 0 2 1 6 *